HOW TO RUN AWAY FROM HOME

HOW TO
RUN AWAY
from
HOME

(And Bring Your Family With You)

ADAM DAILEY

HOW TO RUN AWAY FROM HOME
And Bring Your Family With You

ISBN   978-1-61961-561-8   *Paperback*
        978-1-61961-562-5   *Ebook*

INTERIOR DESIGN BY
Kevin Barrett Kane

LIONCREST
PUBLISHING

ACKNOWLEDGMENTS

I gave some thought to whom I wanted to thank for helping me write this book. But in some sense, I don't feel like I've won an Oscar here. And honestly speaking, most of my inner network of family and friends thought we were crazy for taking this sabbatical.

It would be appropriate to give credit to my family. My parents instilled the adventure of travel in me from an early age. Hearing about their backpacking trips through Belgium, Greece, Italy and Spain always made me interested in what was beyond our borders.

Thanks to my friend and business partner Raffaella, who not only gave me strength and confidence, but also chose to join us in Australia, Spain and Italy. You are family to us.

My children were patient enough to actually participate in this trip, and they were great sports. I hope one day they will thank me. While we missed a year's worth of birthday parties and soccer games, I believe what we gained was so much more.

The person who most deserves a sincere thank you is my wife, Jessica. I had never experienced international travel without her. She is my partner. She is my soulmate. She has stood by me in hard times. And importantly, she didn't laugh at me when I brought up the idea to drop everything and travel around the world. She didn't let logic get in our way. She believed in me. She believed in us. And she continues to be a great mother and role model for our children.

In the end, travel is truly about the people. So maybe I should thank all the different people we encountered on our magical nomadic year. Thanks for showing us around your town, babysitting, letting us sleep in your guest rooms, and having a beer with us while we watched our kids run around that vibrant piazza.

TABLE OF CONTENTS

"People don't take trips, trips take people."

—JOHN STEINBECK

INTRODUCTION

THIS BOOK TELLS THE STORY of my family's year-long sabbatical trip around the world. We said goodbye to our friends and relatives in the United States, and struck out on a great adventure. My wife and lifelong travel partner, Jessica, had four small children at the time, ages one through six. This book is about our adventures—and misadventures—and some of the lessons we learned along the way. But this is also a manifesto of sorts. I firmly believe that taking a year off work and school to travel around the world (with your family) is something everyone can do, and in my opinion, definitely should do. Kids are not an excuse—they're a reason for doing it. It's an incredible gift to your family that they'll benefit from for their whole lives. I'm going to tell you how to do it. The amazing experiences and incredible places we explored are more valuable and educational than years spent sitting in a classroom or an office building working your way up the corporate ladder. We learned so much along the way, and I'm going to share it all with you in the following pages.

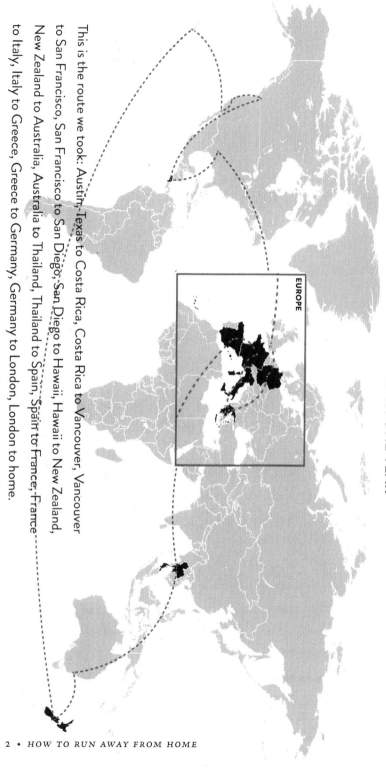

EUROPE

This is the route we took: Austin, Texas to Costa Rica, Costa Rica to Vancouver, Vancouver to San Francisco, San Francisco to San Diego, San Diego to Hawaii, Hawaii to New Zealand, New Zealand to Australia, Australia to Thailand, Thailand to Spain, Spain to France, France to Italy, Italy to Greece, Greece to Germany, Germany to London, London to home.

SIGNIFICANCE OF OUR ROUTE

(it's a bit random to you, but has logic to us):

We chose places that had a personal connection (friends, memories, language, etc.)

1. We selected four places to spend at least month as a homebase (Byron Bay, Sydney, Barcelona and Vancouver).

2. For this trip, we kept it pretty easy. No backpacking in African hostels. Not too many one night stays.

3. To keep luggage easy (and to stay warm), we chose weather that was like "Endless Summer." One light jacket for each kid and heavy on the shorts/t-shirts.

The decision to put life on hold and travel the world is not an easy one. There were many factors that we considered and weighed as we mulled over the idea in our minds. Our oldest child was in school. My business was in a shambles. And it just seemed the timing was never right. Until a series of unfortunate events and costly mistakes led us to conclude that there will never be a good time to go, and there would always be an excuse *not* to go.

"The world is a book, and those who do not travel read only a page."

—SAINT AUGUSTINE

But to fully appreciate this story, you must understand the series of events (you might call some of them unfortunate events) that led us to take the trip of a lifetime. As you will see, we probably had more reasons than anyone *not* to take a trip like this, and definitely not *when* we did it. We had personal and financial obligations, career uncertainty, young children, a child who just started school, a struggling business, massive financial losses, worries about our future, and even a business partner and employees in jail in a foreign country. Believe me, we had more reasons than most families to stay home. But we took off for a year and traveled around the world anyway. Your mind can always come up with reasons not to do this. You'll have to train that part of your brain to shut up.

THIS IS NOT A TRAVELOGUE

Please note that this book is not a travelogue in the traditional sense. We're not going to follow a chronological account of our journey from start to finish. If I were to write a complete journal of our year-long trek around the world, it would fill up 600 pages. Maybe I'll write a book like that about my next sabbatical. The structure of this book is different because its purpose is different. This book is designed to instruct, share, and inspire. I want to show you how to take a sabbatical around the world, and also inspire you to get out of your comfort zone and really do this!

So don't fret if some of the stories are out of order chronologically with our route; many stories have been inserted in order to reinforce key points in the main text. Because the fact is that it really doesn't matter what route you take around the world or which direction you go. Planning your trip of a lifetime is like painting on a blank canvas; there are no right or wrong ways to do it. Whatever appeals to you is just fine. Keep that in mind as you get inspired to create your own sabbatical journey. It will fit to your family, your dreams, your motivations, preferences and passions.

TRAVEL TIPS AND HACKS FOR YOUR SABBATICAL

We learned so much on our trip that I wish we would have known before we left. Most of those lessons are in the pages of this book. So I just want to point a few book elements that will help me tell the story.

At the end of each chapter will be a section titled "Travel Tips and Hacks" in which I'll explain many of the lessons we learned the hard way during our travels with four young children (so you can avoid making the same mistakes).

There are plenty of blogs and books out there offering travel advice, but most of them are designed for young 20-somethings who are single and care-free. There is not much information about doing a year-long sabbatical with young children. So I'll focus on travel tips and hacks for families that I haven't seen explained on other travel sites.

There are also sidebars you'll see throughout the book:

- *Adam's Travel Journal*—Short passages from my journal
- *OMG! Moments*—Odd or challenging situations we found ourselves in
- *LOL! Moments*—Funny things that happened to us along the way
- *Chiara's Journal*—Excepts from my daughter's journal, a different perspective
- *Unforgettable Memories*—Things that we will remember for a lifetime.

And to add in the perspectives of other wise travelers, we've also included some of our favorite travel quotes, from people like Mark Twain, J.R.R. Tolkien, John Steinbeck, and Anthony Kiedis.

HOW IT ALL STARTED

Appropriately enough, the story of our year-long trip around the globe started with the Olympics. In 2003, I received an offer from USA Track and Field to buy tickets to the 2004 Olympic Games in Athens, Greece. I was on their list because I was a former athlete. Jessica and I met in high school through running, in college we were both state NCAA All-Americans. Jessica and I competed at the 2000 U.S. Olympic Trials. So we had a chance to buy tickets to the 2004 Athens Olympics—as many tickets as we wanted.

I had always heard that Olympic tickets were valuable, so even though I didn't have any specific plans in mind, I decided to buy a few thousand dollars worth. "You never know," I told myself, "I could start running again and make the team. And if not, I'll just sell them on eBay." I saw it as an opportunity to make some money. But the truth is that once I got the tickets, I didn't think about them again for nearly a year. My mind was on other things.

I had been involved in sports marketing for a few years at that point, but my career was at a crossroads. As 2004 approached, I was searching for something new. What I really wanted was to find an opportunity that would get me out of Austin, Texas, and back to Europe. Jessica and I had lived in Barcelona for two years prior to moving to Texas, and we loved it. The city was amazing; but just as important, it allowed us to travel all over Europe during that time. And we took full advantage of that. Every free weekend would include a trip to Paris to see Lance Armstrong compete in the Tour de France, or a discounted flight to Dublin to visit friends. But in 2003, we found ourselves stuck in Texas and I was eager for a new adventure.

It's at that moment Jessica and I got an idea that would change the course of our lives for the next decade. "What if we took all these tickets and put together Olympic Tour packages? We could sell people an all-inclusive travel experience including tickets to the games, hotel rooms, airfare, the works." We were so excited about the possibility of our new venture that we decided to spend a few weeks in Greece scouting locations and visiting hotel properties. So without giving it much thought, we packed our bags, and set off for an exploratory trip to Greece at the tail end of 2003.

Any time you arrive in a new country it takes a while to get your bearings, to figure out the quirks and shortcuts that separate the hopeless tourist from the knowledgeable local. By the time most people start to feel comfortable in an unfamiliar country, the trip is over. But we loved this part about traveling. As we roamed around Greece, it occurred to me that I was trying to build a business in the dark; I was thinking about selling travel packages to a place I barely knew. "What if we knew Athens the same way we know Barcelona?" I said to Jessica. "How much value could we bring to people?" She knew instantly what I was hinting at.

Move to Greece? Hmmm. Crazy idea. *Or was it?* I wasn't sure exactly what we would learn or how it would help the business—I just knew that if we made Greece our home we would open up opportunities that just wouldn't come our way living back in Austin. It felt like something we had to consider, or had to *do*.

"It is better to travel well than to arrive."

—BUDDHA

LET'S MOVE TO GREECE

But when our exploratory trip to Greece ended and we landed back in Austin, we had some thinking to do. Making the decision to uproot and move across the world was challenging. I actually had a couple of job offers at the time, including a very attractive offer in Los Angeles, which was probably the safe choice. It would have meant real money and a real career, as opposed to a risky plan to move to Greece with a completely unknown outcome. If we went to Athens, we would have been relying on the ability to sell a bunch of Olympics travel packages, which, by the way, was something I had never done before. I remember telling friends, "We're either going to move to L.A. or Greece." They would just look at me like I'd lost my mind and say, "Well, those sound like pretty different options."

But something was drawing me to Greece. We were young, and I was worried that if I went down a serious career path now I would *never* make it back to Europe—not even to visit—because I'd have just two weeks of vacation a year grinding it out on some corporate treadmill. I feared

I would just fall into the corporate track. Or is it corporate *trap*? Either way, I wasn't ready for that. It felt too serious. Too permanent. I wanted to take a risk. I wanted to jump off the cliff and see where I landed. I knew that someday I would be ready to settle down and do the serious career thing, but not yet. Not now.

I also wanted to test my entrepreneurial chops. I wanted to run a business where I was completely accountable, and where nobody would hold me back.

Jessica understood, and off to Greece we went.

As we did with Barcelona several years prior, we moved straight to Athens not knowing the city or the language. I'm sure that level of uncertainty would fill some people with anxiety (we didn't have a residence set up there until we arrived in Athens and scouted out a few places), but for us, it was an adventure. And we had a blast! We ended up scoring an amazing apartment in a great area of that enormous, pulsing city. The place wasn't furnished, so we bought some used furniture, including a couple of desks, we picked up a used computer courtesy of the Australian Embassy, and soon enough we were in business. We named our business Ludus (in Latin, it means 'game' or 'sport'), and we were on our way to living the good life as ex-pats. At least for a little while.

Initially, our goal was actually pretty modest. Basically, we wanted to create a business that paid all our expenses for the year, and didn't leave us in debt after the Olympics. That's not to say we took the business lightly. We had a very entrepreneurial mindset and we hustled, all day and every day. We emailed everyone we could think of to let them know what we were up to in Athens. We asked for referrals; we tried to connect with anyone and everyone who we thought might be thinking about a trip to Athens for the Olympics.

Unfortunately, our entrepreneurial enthusiasm was soon tested. One of the things we discovered early on is that the hotels we partnered with were at too high of a price point. Most people attending the Olympics are just looking for a cheap place to stay. A low-cost bargain. That was it. So we pivoted. In addition to selling tour packages, we would work as a consultant to find people a hotel or apartment. We would charge a finder's fee between $500 and $1000 and then run around the city looking for places until we located something that suited their needs.

The larger part of our strategy was to add value to our packages by getting to know Athens and using that knowledge to be able to provide our clients the best experience possible. Often that meant insider travel tips and hacks like, "Take this metro line, not that one," or "Don't go to this restaurant because it's a tourist trap." That gave us a big advantage over tour companies that weren't located in Greece. We also had an advantage over the Greek travel companies because we not only were located in Athens, but we also were native English speakers. We were Americans, which we soon realized made our American clients worry less about being taken advantage of or ripped off by a foreign company.

The sad fact is that Greece has a reputation for trying to screw over tourists. Jessica and I went to a restaurant one time and they tried to overcharge us by ten times the price that the locals pay. When we complained they tried to tell us "No, that's not a decimal point. It's not 7 euros, it's 70 euros." Apparently, that's a typical scam throughout Greece. We helped our guests avoid situations like that.

Tourists also had to be vigilant with the taxi drivers. Maneuvering cabs is a sport in Athens. You have to know exactly how much you're paying and what they can charge you. Every cab ride we took became a negotiation. In fact, taxis in Athens will pick up 2-3 people (like Uber Pool) based on your destination, which you must yell out as they slow down and deliberate on whether or not to pick up that person. The best way to solve this nuisance was to make friends with some of the locals and hang out with them, because then the cabbies knew not to try to pull a fast one on fellow Athenians. Shouting is also a sport in Greece (and completely acceptable).

We used many of these same lessons—which we learned the hard way—to help out our clients once the Olympics began. When we were hanging out with our customers, they felt like family. We loved showing them around 'our city'.

I've always been a pretty entrepreneurial person, but this was my first real business, and I was operating off of pure hustle. In my past jobs, one of the things that frustrated me was promising something to a customer and then not being able to deliver because of my co-workers or boss. I loved being in a position where I was the boss, where I could say, "Here's what I'm going to do," and then do it. I loved working for myself. I loved the freedom. And I loved living abroad.

Of course, running our own company also came with plenty of fear and anxiety. I had no backstop, no safety net, and I did *not* want to fail. There were many nights when I would look at the clock, see that it was 8:00 pm, and I would want to take a break. But I knew I had to keep going, keep working. I just had to succeed. It was an exhilarating mix of fun and fear and hope, all set in an exotic city that was hosting a world-class sporting event. And I loved it.

I mentioned that in a past life I had run track, and I think that one thing about our business model that really appealed to me was that there was a start and a finish line. After the Olympics ended, that was it; our business would also end. It was finite. Our success was measurable: what was left in our bank account the day after the Closing Ceremonies. Plus, even though we worked hard, the finish line made the demands of the workload bearable because we knew we weren't going to be stuck in overdrive mode forever. We just had to make it through the Olympics. And if, after all the dust had settled, we had some money left over, we saw it as a bonus. It was an amazing learning experience for us, and an adventure.

"I never travel without my diary. One should always have something sensational to read on the train."

—OSCAR WILDE

Our business grew fast. We ended up bringing over a couple employees from the United States (who happened to be my sister and her best friend). We housed them in our 2 bedroom apartment and gave them a salary of 100 euros a week in the beginning. Then we brought over a few more team members (Australians/Americans) about a month before the Olympics started. We were on a roll. The business was generating revenue. And we had an amazing Olympics experience overall. By the end of our time in Greece, not only did we avoid losing money and going into debt, we actually turned a profit of more than $30,000. That was a lot of money for us at the time. Heck, that's a lot of money for anyone. As we sipped a glass of retsina wine in a sidewalk café I thought to myself, "This is success."

We were on top of the world. But it wouldn't last forever.

RINSE AND REPEAT

After we closed up shop in Athens, we decided that we needed a vacation. We got our final month of rent for free in exchange for leaving behind all the furniture we had purchased. So we used a good chunk of the money we made to spend the rest of 2004 traveling through Spain and Italy. One of the stops happened to be Torino, Italy, the site of the upcoming 2006 Winter Olympics. We enjoyed spending time in Torino, and made the decision to move there at the beginning of 2005. This was a risk. We didn't speak Italian. And we knew nothing about the Winter Olympics. I had grown up waterskiing in Texas!

We stayed in Torino, running our business, for over a year, until March 2006. We had five full-time employees in Torino, and we had generated about $1.5 million in sales for the 2006 Winter Olympic Games.

Then we moved straight to Germany and set up shop for the 2006 FIFA World Cup soccer tournament. At this point we had really figured out the sporting events business and we felt like we were on a roll. Plus we loved taking time off to travel after working really hard for so long. In October 2006, we flew to Santiago, Chile, and spent the rest of the year traveling through Chile, Ecuador, Peru, Guatemala, Mexico and Costa Rica. *Are you beginning to see a pattern here?* Travel was so much a part of our professional and personal lives we felt totally at home not having a place to call home. We loved seeing exotic new places and meeting interesting people. But we also never felt grounded. We never had a home; maybe we were constantly looking for something. Maybe we were just being flexible.

After the holidays in 2006, we took another extended trip to Australia, where we would spend the next several months and conceive our first child! We had planned to move to Paris after our Australia trip and get set up for the 2007 Rugby World Cup. But we made a last minute decision to return to Barcelona. We knew the city. We spoke Spanish. We had a social network. And we could get to Pamplona and Munich pretty easily—two places where we were hosting clients that summer.

We also figured we should focus on the upcoming Beijing Olympics more than the Rugby World Cup (an event we knew nothing about). And with our first child coming we knew we would feel more comfortable in the thriving Catalan city. So we moved back to Barcelona in May 2007, where we would spend the rest of the year. On November 4, 2007, we welcomed our first child, Chiara Shay Dailey.

"Everyone wants to ride with you in the limo, but what you want is someone who will take the bus with you when the limo breaks down."

—OPRAH WINFREY

In January 2008, we left Barcelona to move back to North America. We had a small team based in Beijing, and we wanted to ensure we were preparing for the Olympics in Vancouver, Canada. We decided to move there without ever even having visited! We thought Vancouver would be a great place to live. It was close to home, but still a foreign country. Not only would be beneficial for us to be based there for our business, but also it was one of the most beautiful cities we'd ever seen. We spent the next three years in Vancouver, growing our business and our family. Our first son, Jett, was born in October 2009, just a few months before the upcoming Winter Olympics.

Also, we weren't excited about Beijing (or the pollution) as a city. The Vancouver Games were great for us. The event was profitable. We made a bunch of money. We had a good team in place, and I was poised to really take our business to the next level...in San Diego. *What could possibly go wrong?* Little did we know that something was about to go down that would jeopardize everything and test us on every level.

LONDON: $10 MILLION OPPORTUNITY OR DISASTER?

In 2010, we continued our business model of offering travel packages to major sporting events around the world. It worked, and it was a blast. We moved our growing family to San Diego, and I really wanted to expand the business. I had a couple people approach me about buying the company, Ludus. But potential suitors would always point that they thought what I had was more of a lifestyle business; one that revolved around my contacts, experiences and personality. So it became apparent that I had to create a business that revolved more around systems and processes, and less around my ability to create deals. My objective was to make it scalable—to create a business that could grow big and didn't depend solely on Jessica and me (and our contacts). So I began working to expand the company. Our goal was to generate more than $10 million in revenue for the 2012

Olympics in London. We had banners made. Every single employee was set to receive some kind of bonus if we hit that number.

Unfortunately, things don't always go the way you want them to.

Here's what happened. In order to close $10 million in sales we had to go big. And we had to invest big. We purchased more than 5,000 Olympic tickets in advance (bought at an average of more than $400 each). That is more tickets than the Olympic Committees from countries like Vietnam and Chile receive. It was also a couple million dollars in expenses. We also booked about 400 hotel rooms, and each booking was for 18 nights. That was our inventory, and the plan was to completely sell out. But I made three mistakes that would prove costly.

"Sometimes things have to go wrong in order to go right."

—SHERRILYN KENYON

The first mistake was that I didn't take into account the fact that London basically has a dozen hotels on every block (not to mention a growing Airbnb inventory). So many hotels! I also failed to consider that since London is an English-speaking city, Americans generally felt comfortable shopping around and booking hotels on their own. It wasn't like Athens or Beijing where people were leery about ending up in the wrong neighborhood or getting scammed by an overseas operator. Everyone could communicate just fine. Heck, it even seemed like half the people had a friend or distant relative in London ready to let them crash on the floor.

The second mistake I made compounded the first. I was so busy trying to grow the company—trying to hire people, motivate people, and drum up new business—that I didn't have my finger on the pulse of the company as much as I had in the past. I wasn't paying attention to the fact that the Games were fast approaching and we weren't moving our inventory. Big problem.

And the last mistake, I decided to build my $10 million business with a team of rookies. They were good people, mind you, but a rag-tag team of 20+ employees who had no Olympic or event experience whatsoever. This proved to be the nail in the coffin.

Part of the challenge was that I was getting undercut on price by the same hotels I was trying to sell to my clients. For example, I had bought 80% of a hotel's inventory and paid them $500 a night two years in advance. Then, as the Olympics approached, they would start selling whatever remained of the 20 percent of the rooms that I hadn't booked for just $250 a night online. I'd tell them, "You're killing me. You can't do this." But they sure could. And they did. Plus, the people of London didn't really seem to care about the Olympics. The people were cold, and ultimately, the Olympics had disappointed them.

"The path with no obstacles usually leads nowhere."

—JESSICA DAILEY

I would tell potential clients, "This is a cute hotel, in a great location—it's a great opportunity for you." Then the client would Google the hotel and say, "Perfect. You sold me on the hotel, but unfortunately I'm going to take the $250 price rather than the $600 you want to charge me." Ouch. Overloaded with inventory I couldn't sell, I became desperate. I started telling customers, "Fine, I'll sell it to you for $250." My team would be celebrating that we had $250, but I felt like crying because I knew I was losing half my money. I was taking a 50-percent loss, yet we were relieved because it wasn't a 100-percent loss. Our business definition of a 'win' became a moving target.

Soon enough, I saw the writing on the wall. A month and a half before the Olympics I realized we were going to lose a huge amount of money. It was only a matter of how much. I had a panic attack. It was the first panic attack of my life. I remember thinking, "Oh my God. This is going to be really bad." From then on, our goal was to aggressively maximize revenue any way we could in order to minimize the horrible loss that was coming our way.

Like I said, our original goal was to reach $10 million in revenue. We ended up with $7 million—one million dollars less than our break-even point. Yes, I lost a million dollars in less than 20 days. It was brutal. I had put about $600,000 of my own money into the business, plus a $250,000 line of credit that was maxed out by the time of the event. I still owed vendors and credit card companies hundreds of thousands of dollars. And here we were, a million dollars in the hole. London was obviously the not the goldmine I had envisioned for the past couple of years.

Big global events are always hard in this business. It's very stressful and there are endless complaints and other challenges you have to deal with. That's tolerable when you're making money. But try handling all that stress and those complaints when you're losing a fortune! The 2012 Olympics turned out to be the worst two weeks of my life. It still hurts to think about it.

BACK HOME AND DEPRESSED

As the London Games came to a close, I returned to San Diego and felt like crawling into a hole. We had to fire 1/3 of our team before they even left England. I've always been a positive person. I've always been successful, both as a competitive athlete and later in business. I had never really failed at anything before. This was my first severe ass-kicking, and it hurt. Bad. That hurt was amplified because it rode in on the coattails of what had been enormous hope and optimism.

Prior to London, I felt like I was on this amazing journey to success. I had been telling Jessica, "I'm working so hard for London because things will be different afterwards. We're going to buy a bigger house. I'm going to step away from the business and focus on other pursuits." I painted this picture of how amazing life was going to be with the influx of seven-figures of profit.

I had planned on life being different after London. It certainly was. Just not in the way I had planned!

Instead of moving into a bigger house, we started looking for a more affordable one. For the first time in my life, I had to go on antidepressants. Jessica wasn't feeling sorry for me, either. She resented the fact that I was somewhat reckless with our financial situation and had lost a huge part of our net worth. I was feeling sorry for myself, while she thought, "I'm not going to sit here and help you wallow. Get up and figure out what we do next." As she recalls:

> I was uneasy as the company grew to 25 employees, overhead was high and the company kept buying and more London inventory. I kept trying to tell Adam "enough" but he was set on pushing forward.

My plan was to sell the business. A year before the London Games I had an offer for about $2 million that didn't go through, although looking back on it maybe I could have pushed it through. Now here I was trying to sell the business for practically nothing—just to pay off the debt I had on it. I just wanted out.

"If the road is easy, you're likely going the wrong way."

—TERRY GOODKIND

By the end of 2013, I had a buyer for the business lined up. Pablo (not his real name) had created one of the most successful ticketing businesses in history. He was rebuilding. He offered to take on my debt and give me equity in his new venture. But he was a jerk. He belittled me—and my staff. I knew he'd eat me up and spit me out.

But at the end of the day, I didn't care. I just wanted to get out from the debt, from the mounting pressure I was facing daily. And in November of 2012, in the midst of all of this complete chaos, we got pregnant with our fourth child. This did not simplify life.

I explained my deal to my good friend in Austin, who ran a similar but complementary business. He reasoned, "Don't sell it. We should go into business together."

So in April 2013, I officially sold my business, and as a result, became partners with my long-time friend. On the bright side, our businesses combined had a lot of revenue, but the struggle was on the profit side. There were a lot of problems we had to fix. And our future success would hinge on the 2014 World Cup in Brazil.

My new business partner was living in Austin and he convinced me to move there as we prepared for Brazil. "Our chances of success will go up exponentially if we're in the same place every day," he argued. I was still reeling from London. And to make matter worse, I had all kinds of lawsuits mounting against me—ranging from an employee to a vendor to a client. This caused a considerable amount of stress, paranoia and anxiety. I was tired and beaten down. So I thought, "Maybe what I need is a fresh start." Besides, I'm *from* Austin! Both of Jessica's and my family still lived in town. I figured it might be just what I needed, to take a break from San Diego and the life I had built there. Get out of Dodge and figure out what's next.

> "When you travel, remember that a foreign country is not designed to make you comfortable. It is designed to make its own people comfortable."
>
> —CLIFTON FADIMAN

A lot had changed since we started Ludus back in 2003. For one thing, Jessica and I now had four young children. A strange consequence of my growing family was that travel was now something that induced anxiety (instead of giving me joy like it once had). I was never comfortable leaving

Jessica alone for days with the kids while I was away on business.

That wasn't the only reason I no longer enjoyed traveling for work. Travel reinforced the fact that I was no longer happy in my business. London had simply taken too much of a toll on me. I was burned out, both professionally and personally.

All of this was going through my mind as I took a trip to Pensacola, Florida, for a business conference. I sat on the plane with frayed nerves and anxiety pumping through my veins. During my first day, I got strep throat. And adding to my stress, I figured I would see partners from London; perhaps they were still mad about how things had gone during the London Olympics. *"Why am I doing this?"* I thought to myself. *"I'm miserable."*

THE IDEA TO TAKE A ONE-YEAR SABBATICAL

So I'm sitting on the plane heading to Florida, with all of these negative thoughts and fears bouncing around my head. Then I start flipping through one of those airline magazines in the seat pocket. I found myself looking at the various destinations in the pages. That's when I pulled out a notebook and started scribbling down notes.

What's wrong with me? What do I love? I want to be with my family. I'm not happy in San Diego. I'm not happy in Austin. I used to love traveling, but I don't even *like* traveling anymore. Why don't I like traveling? It's stressful when I leave my family. It's stressful when I'm traveling with my family. It's hard to move around with four kids. *What if there was some solution here?*

At that moment, something clicked. I had this vision: a year-long trip around the world with my family. A break. A sabbatical, where I would leave the business behind and simply see the world with Jessica and children. I started flipping through the American Airlines magazine, studying the routes and building a travel window and an itinerary in my head. "What if I could do this?" I thought. *"What if I just left the stress of the business behind and take my family with me?"*

When I got home from the Pensacola trip I told Jessica about my wacky idea. Anyone else's wife would have said, "We have four small children. You're freaking crazy!" But her response was different. She was excited by the idea. But she was also reluctant. "I don't think you're really ready to pull the trigger on something like this."

In part, she was right. The logical part of my brain had its doubts. But in my heart I really was committed to the trip. And we soon started putting together our itinerary and planning flights. But before we could actually pack our bags and hit the road, I had to deal with the matter of Brazil—the 2014 FIFA World Cup.

THE BRAZIL DISASTER

When my new partner and I merged our businesses, we both thought we were going to make a ton of money off of the World Cup. We were focused more on how to divide up profits than we were on how to streamline a successful business venture. And I was eager to recoup some of my losses from London. But as things got closer we started to realize that we weren't going to get rich in Brazil. Nevertheless, we figured we would do okay, pay off some debt, and put the business on sound financial footing going forward.

We were very much looking forward to that. Unfortunately, we were soon getting our asses kicked. Every month we had to cover $250,000 of overhead; and we could never get ahead of it. By the time we made payroll, paid for our offices, paid licensing fees to our various partners… we would end up broke at the end of every month.

It was an interesting time, I learned a lot, and I definitely benefited from having a good partner with whom I could share my struggles. But it was not a fun time. The lack of success was a constant drain—financially and psychologically. I felt more like an employee than a business owner. I felt like I was driving to *work* every day, a sensation I hadn't felt in more than a decade. It made me even more convinced that I had to get out and take my sabbatical trip.

There was still a lot to do. We had opened up an office in Brazil, and on the bright side, things were going significantly better than they had in London. But the fact is we were underprepared. When I went down to our office where we had five employees, it was clear that two or three of them hadn't done their jobs for the past year. They were living the Brazilian lifestyle and doing their best for the company, but they'd gone unchecked. At the end of the day, even that responsibility probably ended up with me.

But that wasn't the disaster.

"Though we travel the world over to find the beautiful, we must carry it with us or we find it not."

—RALPH WALDO EMERSON

On June 30, 2014, we were in the middle of the World Cup, in full-on event mode and working around the clock. It was about halfway through the World Cup when we had some unexpected visitors come to our hospitality area in Copacabana. Undercover police raided us! Well, at least we were *hoping* they were police. They stormed in carrying guns but without showing us any badges. And this being Brazil, we feared the very real possibility someone was going to get killed. Thankfully, it turns out that they were, in fact, the police. But they were crooked cops. They were accusing my partner of illegally selling tickets. Sidenote: scalping (selling a ticket for more than its face value) is illegal in Brazil. In theory, the offense could carry jail time. While the purchases had all been carried out back home in the USA (where it was legal), we were about to find out that logic wouldn't play a huge part in Brazilian law.

So there we were in our office, being held at gunpoint, surrounded by World Cup tickets and bags of cash. It didn't look good. My partner agreed to go with them to the police station to sort out the situation. But then one of the officers got the idea to search our bags. They unzipped our duffel bags and found a boatload of tickets and $25,000 in cash (in about four different currencies, which they found fascinating). The police claimed we were running some huge illegal ticket scalping operation, and started demanding that we all go with them down to the police station.

I told them that I did nothing wrong, that the cash was to pay our tour guides, and that no way was I coming with them to the station. "I've done nothing wrong," I boldly argued. I knew getting into that police car would be a mistake. One of the police pulled me aside and explained loudly, "Here's the deal. If you don't come with us to the station, I'm going to keep the money. If you come with us, you'll get the cash back."

I was in a tough position. I did not want to go to the police station, because I didn't know if I'd ever get out of there. But I was also standing in front of some of my employees, and I had to project leadership and strength in front of them. So, finally, I said, "I'll go with you. I've done nothing wrong." They took a picture of my partner's and my driver's licenses, and they walked us down to the lobby of the hotel.

My partner could barely make eye contact with me. Earlier that day I had warned him about bringing in so many tickets to the office at once—we had about a million dollars' worth at that point—because I was terrified of getting robbed. I literally picked up the tickets and started to take them out of the office. "Stop. I'm the ticket guy," he argued. "You're the travel guy. Don't touch the tickets. Put them back." As we were standing in the lobby he just turned to me and said, "I'm so sorry." I was so angry I couldn't acknowledge him.

This would be the last time I would see him for more than a year.

What happened next was truly unbelievable. As we were walking out of the hotel, a common street thief tried to rob a bus right in front of this circus of police that had taken over the large hotel lobby. So the six or seven cops who were with us ran after him and started beating him up and handcuffed him. My partner looked at me like, "What should we do?" There was a ton of commotion. Then one of the cops came back and grabbed my partner and put him in a police car. Another police officer got into his car and drove away. But I was left just standing there, by myself, twelve feet from the glass lobby door. I just stood there and watched as the police got in their cars and took off without me.

What the hell just happened? I stood still for a moment not knowing what to do. But I quickly decided that I was *not* going to turn myself in. I was *not* going to the police station. I was *not* going to spend the night in a Brazilian jail. So I went back inside the hotel, went upstairs to the office, quickly grabbed my personal belongings, and told the remaining staff that I was going out for a walk.

The police had taken a bunch of our cash, they had taken essentially all of our tickets, and now my partner was in jail. I was trying to sort things out in my head and figure out my next move. I was panicked. How could everything go so wrong so quickly? An hour later I got a call from someone on my team—she was my best and most loyal employee. But more than that, she was like a sister to me. She said, "the police are here again. They realized they forgot you." There was a long pause. "They want you to come back." She said, "They want me to go with them."

I think we both knew this was a bad deal for her. We both realized the world isn't a fair place. She hadn't touched a ticket during the entire World Cup. And here she was, being taken to the police station. She was later charged with racketeering. I felt horrible, and didn't know what to do. I just told her, "Well, I'm not coming back."

For the next few days, I was basically on the run in Brazil. The police had a copy of my ID, and apparently went back to our host hotel looking for me. My family kept telling me I needed to get out of the country while I could. So did our Board of Directors. And pretty much everyone I knew.

I relented. I was scared. I couldn't eat or sleep. I figured I wasn't doing anyone any good as long as I was scared about my personal freedom. As I told a couple key employees about my departure, one cried. Another turned pale. They thought I was abandoning them. I guess, in the literal sense, I was.

As I arrived at the airport to check in, I was drenched in sweat. I didn't care. I kept looking for body language from the American Airlines rep checking me in. Then I had to pass through customs. "This was it," I thought to myself. I looked at his computer screen, fully expecting it to start flashing red and for guards to pounce on me. Didn't happen. I sat waiting for the flight to board. My phone reception was spotty. They must have jammed my signal, I thought.

I got on the plane, and fully expected agents to come on the plane and yank me off, as they'd done a couple years later with the American swimmers at the Rio Olympics. It felt like the final scenes from the movie *Argo*. When the wheels went up, I felt a sense of relief.

TIME FOR A CHANGE

I felt terribly guilty for fleeing the country. But I also had visions of spending years in a Brazilian prison for evading police and resisting arrest. My friend and another key employee were now in jail. My partner was arrested and charged. The police said that my partner was scalping tickets, and they were going to charge our employees with racketeering. Under Brazilian law, if you arrest more than two people doing anything illegal, the police consider it organized crime. It was apparent that the police went back to the hotel to arrest my employees just to make this happen.

I spent every waking moment trying to get them out. We also spent most of our cash, including a $20,000 cash drop in the middle of the night to pay a lawyer, and $50,000 to pay a judge. The police kept most of the $25,000 they confiscated; new reports claimed they had caught us with only $9,000 (and you can conclude what happened to the other $16,000).

After five days, they were sent to prison. Yes, prison. Bangu, to be exact. Google that place; it's not a resort.

After two weeks they were all released. But the government kept their passports and they were stuck in Brazil for three more months. Then the Brazilian police shook us down one last time. Before they finally agreed to let everyone leave the country they said, "Either you let us keep the cash here and plead no contest, or we'll have to delay this one more month." Everyone wanted to clear their names and show they were innocent. But by that point they basically said, "Forget it. I don't care what I have to sign. Just let me out of here."

Meanwhile, as all of this legal drama was unfolding, I was still trying to run our World Cup event from the United States. My three main employees at the event were completely taken out by the police. So I was running the World Cup operation with almost no support. This was more than just difficult. It was never ending. I was putting out fires with clients and employees all day, while trying to get the Rio Trio out of jail and calling anyone I could think of. It was definitely one of the most stressful periods of my life.

I was fried. But I was more than just burned out. I hated this job. I hated this industry. I vowed to never put my family in this position again, and to never put myself in this position. I needed to get away, to run away. The sabbatical seemed like the way to go.

The date that Jessica and I had tentatively put on the calendar for the family sabbatical was less than a month away, and I recall Jessica asking me whether we were going. At first I told her, "We can't go if they're still in jail in Brazil." Even after they were released, I still figured there was no way I could go so long as there continued to be legal complications in Brazil. I figured the business would need me, not to mention the guilt I still continued to carry.

But my colleagues knew about the sabbatical I was planning with my family. Everyone in our company knew I had been wanting to get out of the business for quite a while. And they knew that I had grown more eager to leave given the disaster that was now taking place in South America. I felt like George Bailey in *It's a Wonderful Life*—always being sucked back into a life I didn't want for myself. In the end, they supported my decision to go on the trip. I felt like I was abandoning my partner. Yet from his perspective, my leaving actually had an upside—I would be taking a huge pay cut. Our business was on life support. So by removing my salary, it would leave more capital on our balance sheet, thus giving the company a higher chance of survival.

So I decided to keep pushing forward. My family and I needed this. Jessica and I were packing up our four children and we were going on a one-year sabbatical—a trip around the world. *But where to begin? Where to go? What to see? Would it be safe traveling with the children? What about doctors and school?* So many questions swirled around our heads as we finalized our plans.

But we knew we wanted to do this, we were committed to it, and we believed we could solve any problem that came up. To be honest, I just wanted to get off the grid; I wanted to escape, and I needed time to lick my wounds. We also believed it would be the best year of all of our lives.

Were we right? Read on to find out.

TRAVEL TIPS AND HACKS

Calculate Your Current Expenses

One of the important messages of this book is that you can often do extended travel abroad for about the same cost as living at home (especially in North America) and sometimes a lot less. If you plan it right, go to less expensive countries, aggressively collect airline miles and credit card points for a few years in advance, and rent out your home, you should be able to do this. And you wouldn't even have to sell any of your stuff either. We went for a full year, but there is no rule that you have to go for that long. A six-month sabbatical would be less than half the cost, and would provide almost as much of an adventure. Heck, three or four months of international travel would also be amazing and would satisfy almost any size travel bug. Your trip is what you make of it. And whether you go for six months, a year, or two years, I know you're going to have the time of your life. So keep reading, and start thinking creatively about how you're going to make your own sabbatical happen. You can do it.

Airline and Hotel Points

As I discussed earlier in this book, airline and hotel points can be accumulated for several years before you leave on your sabbatical. It's smart to study your credit cards and figure out which ones give the most points for which types of purchases. You always want to maximize your points by using the best card for each use. Some cards give triple points on gasoline. Some give double points on groceries. Figure this out and work it to your advantage. Over a few years this can really add up. I use a website/blog called The Points Guy (ThePointsGuy.com). Sites like this walk you through the best way to maximize your points and to make sure they don't expire. This strategy alone can make your sabbatical affordable.

I used to fly a lot of different airlines for my tour business. But then I started booking everything on American Airlines because I wanted to maximize my points in one place. I would even fly at odd times and take longer legs to get more points.

And here's one thing that really put me into the super bonus round with my points. I started using my credit cards to pay vendors to my business. In other words, I used my credit cards—instead of checks—to pay large business expenses just so I could rack up the points and miles. Often the vendors did not want to accept credit card payment because of the 2-3% processing fee. But I would insist, "If you want my business this is how I need to pay." It worked almost every time. Sometimes, only if the vendor refused, I'd offer to split the 2.5% fee with them. I have asked vendors to charge a credit card for more than $70,000 more times than I can recall. That resulted in 70,000 points that I could use toward a free international flight or hotel stay.

Maximize Your Points

In 2006, Jessica and I showed up to Oslo to pick up World Cup tickets. The value of the tickets was close to $1 million. They were expecting that I was bringing the remaining balance ($250k) in cash. They were more than surprised (and maybe a little frustrated) when I brought out 10 different credit cards and had them charge various amounts to each card. But I walked out with a stack of tickets and 250,000 more points.

Anyone can do this. If you pay tuition to your kid's school, ask if you can set up automatic billing on your credit card. Then sit back and watch the miles pile up. If you shop at Costco, don't pay with a check or a debit card. Get the Costco credit card and you'll earn triple points on all Costco purchases. You can even buy travel through Costco on your Costco card and earn points back on your travel which you can use to buy more travel. If I could find a way to pay my mortgage with a credit card I'd do it. (I'm actually going to look into that!)

Local SIM Cards and Skype

International cell phone bills can put you in the poor house fast. But you don't need to blow your budget just to stay connected to loved ones back home. First step is to just cut your local contract.

Trust me. They might make you 'pause' it for $5 a month until the contract period ends. We found great deals on local SIM cards throughout our travels. We found a prepaid card for $40 a month in Australia with unlimited calls within Australia, 2 GB of data, and even unlimited calls to the USA and Australia). This saved us a ton. We couldn't imagine the cost of using a United States SIM card. As of the time of this writing, international calling plans are changing. And phone technology is changing. So the point is to do your research before you leave on your trip. Don't just accept whatever high-priced international plan is offered by AT&T or Verizon. If you shop around you can do better.

But ultimately, you'll want to unlock your phone and buy local SIM cards with data wherever you go. We also bought a local U.S. Skype phone number and forwarded our calls coming from the USA to our local SIM phone. In most of the world, incoming calls are free. So our friends and family could call a local U.S. number and it would get transferred via Skype directly to our cell phone in whatever country we were in. Whenever we'd arrive in a new country, we would change the forwarding to our new local number. There might be a slight delay in the connection, but only a few seconds. The calls sounded great. At that time, Skype charged us about two cents per minute. So we could talk for an hour for $1.20. Not bad. And to all of our friends back home it was all transparent, it just seemed to then like they were calling a local U.S. phone number.

Keep a Journal

I believe it's vital to keep a journal. You should chronicle as much as you can, whether it's expenses, names of restaurants, or the addresses of the houses you are renting. A good journal will help jog your memory long after your trip. It's about taking notes. For me, it was also about writing down my feelings. I wrote about things that would happen every day.

At times, I wouldn't be able to write in my journal for several days. Or I would just jot down a non-emotional recollection of what our schedule had been. That's fine. Just write. And when you're creative, you can come back and fill in the gaps later. But having a chronicle of your travels that can complement your photos and your social media is going to be really important to you one day. I promise that you won't remember the name of that restaurant in Seville five years from now. But if you have it written down, you're in business!

By the end of the trip, my journal was a living, breathing document that was more than 200 pages. I recommend you do the same.

"Twenty years from now you will be more disappointed by the things you didn't do than by the ones you did. So throw off the bowlines, sail away from the safe harbor, catch the trade winds in your sails. Explore. Dream. Discover."

—MARK TWAIN

1. FINDING THE RIGHT TIME TO GO
(Hint: There Isn't One)

WHEN I TELL PEOPLE about my year-long family sabbatical, the response is always the same. They say, "I could never do that," or, "I don't have the money, or the job flexibility." I would respond with examples of my similar struggles. "My kids are too young, or my kids are too old." Well, if anyone had a valid excuse not to pull the trigger and take a trip of this magnitude, it was I. I had friends asking me, "You're really going to leave your business partner when he needs you the most?" I had four young children. I was depressed. And my business was falling apart. Not ideal conditions for this kind of momentous trip.

But the way I looked at it was, *there's always going to be some excuse not to go.* Whether it's your children being too young or too old, or your business partner getting thrown in prison in Brazil, or you can't leave your job or your business, there will always be a reason why you can't pack your bags and go see the world. You have to ask yourself if this is something you are committed to do.

For me, it definitely was. It was something that I not only wanted to do, it was something I *had* to do. Did I have doubts? Of course! But we disregarded all the reasons *not* to do it, and we just made the leap. And you can too.

You might wonder why I made that decision when most people wouldn't have. My dad was a business owner who ran his own deck company, and I was very entrepreneurial growing up. I was always buying and selling stuff, trying to make extra cash. Money was important to me, and truth be told, I never really questioned why. By the time I was mid-way through building my events business, I had more than I needed. I was hooked on making money. And it was only when I started questioning that—when I started to see that I had more than enough for the lifestyle I wanted to live—that I was able to formulate the idea of the sabbatical.

But what kind of life *did* I want to live? I remember my parents talking about their trips to Europe and all their other travel experiences. It seemed so exotic and exciting, far more than the middle class lifestyle I was enjoying on a day to day level.

✐ ADAM'S TRAVEL JOURNAL

During the kids' naps I would usually try to get some work done, but it's much harder than I thought. I am having much less 'free time' than I anticipated. During this trip I wanted to read, write, and rediscover myself. Well, cleaning and parenting and having fun is a full time job, not to mention our actual trip and the planning that is going into it. I guess I'll work some other time.

Jessica, by the way, had similarly romanticized European travel growing up. She spent a summer in Sweden when she was 13 years old, which she said was a highlight of her childhood. For both of us, Europe—and travel in general—held a certain allure. But if you've read this far you already knew that. We were about to step on the gas pedal…big time.

KEY POINT

That was the big insight that propelled us to take the trip; *I was willing to accept a diminished net worth in exchange for memories that would last a lifetime.* I could justify losing thousands of dollars every month if it meant a once-in-a-lifetime experience of traveling with my family, to really connect with them, and to do the things I *wanted* to do instead of the things I thought I *had* to do.

Here's another line of thought that was going through my mind. I would tell myself, "I'm bringing home $10,000 a month after taxes. Man, that's a lot of money to not be enjoying my life. If you gave me $10,000 cash at the beginning of this next 30 days, I would not choose to do this life that I'm doing." The next question that would inevitably be asked was, "What would you do with that $10,000?" And my answer didn't waver much from, "Some kind of travel."

I also thought about it this way: yes, there are a million reasons why this is crazy, a million reasons why this was the wrong time to do it. But just as there is never a perfect time to have children and you do it anyway because it's important to you, I decided to follow through because of its importance to me. Sure, there was a temptation to wait until things were more stable, to wait until the kids were older, to wait until we had an ever larger financial cushion. Or to wait until I had a "4-Hour Work Week" on auto-pilot ready to spin off cash. But the longer you postpone the trip of a lifetime the less likely you are to do it. A mantra within the Facebook corporate culture is that, "Done is better than perfect."

Let that settle in.

In the final analysis, the question I asked myself was, "Is there any chance if we pull the trigger now that we'll end up regretting this five, ten, or twenty years later?" I thought, "I can't see that. I don't regret a single travel experience from the past—not even a little bit." And shortly thereafter the decision was made. We're doing this.

That's how I encourage people to think about taking their own sabbatical. Stop asking whether it's the right *time*, and start asking, *"If I did it, would I look back and regret it?"* That can really be a life-changing perspective. And only you can answer that question. And the further out you want to plan your trip, the higher the likelihood is that things will occur in your life that prevent you from going. As John Lennon put it, "life is what happens you while you're busy making other plans."

✎ ADAM'S TRAVEL JOURNAL

Returning our rental cars was often a surreal experience. One time, in Nosara, Costa Rica, they claimed I brought the car back with less gas. But I had a photo to prove I didn't. We argued. Then they said I had damaged the car. This car was beat to hell when we got it. We went outside and inspected it. The guy started to crawl *under* the vehicle to show me damage under the car. I said, "You mean, as I'm getting the rental car, I'm supposed to crawl underneath the car and look at everything to make sure it's ok?" I asked him in Spanish. As he glanced over at his colleague, he knew the whole thing was ridiculous. We headed back inside.

FINANCING THE TRIP

Of course, that didn't mean there weren't practical considerations to worry about. The fact of the matter was, we had to figure out a way to afford it, or minimize our losses. The first issue was cash. The business agreed to pay me $3,000 a month to consult, which was nice, but it was nearly an 80% pay cut. We saved a few bucks. We sold our cars. We sold our beds. We sold everything we could, from baby strollers to toys. Cash trumped everything. Basically, we got to the point where we hoped we could make it through the year-long trip without running out of money. And we knew that if worse came to worst, we could make up the difference with credit cards. In the end, I simply had faith that whatever happened, I would figure something out.

One strategy we used was renting out our house and two other pieces of property we owned. The home we had spent the last year living in had tenants for the next 12 months. We wouldn't generate any positive cash flow from it, but ultimately, it would likely break even. I was just happy we wouldn't have to think about it much. The other properties we rented out through Airbnb. This gave us a very unique perspective on using the Airbnb platform over the next year. We became 'power users' because we were both a renter and an owner.

The other thing that really helped was cashing in my many frequent flier miles. I had millions of miles because I had put so many of our business expenses, hotels, travel, meals, employee meals, etc., on airline credit cards. And once I knew I was going to do the round the world trip, I used the cards more strategically and more often. This is something I recommend to anyone planning a similar trip. Maximize your frequent flier points in the year leading up to your departure. Study how your cards award points, and use the right card for the right expense to maximize your miles. If you get creative there are dozens of ways you can get airline miles. I know people who have worked out a deal with their landlords to pay their rent on a credit card so they can get the corresponding miles.

To summarize, our financial strategy was based on:

- renting out our home (trying to break even, although positive cash flow would've been nice)
- renting out some other properties (short term; we needed a local property manager)
- $3,000 per month in living expenses from my business
- utilizing frequent flyer miles, and credit cards to absorb any overages if we ran out of money before the end of the trip.

It was going to be tight, but we were hopeful we could make it work. And a lot of our decision was based on the notion that we could probably do this trip and actually live for less money than we spend in our normal life. That was a big part of my overall hypothesis—that we could spend less traveling than we would spend at home. When you're in your daily and weekly routine back home there are hundreds of expenses that you don't have while traveling. Dry cleaning, car payments, gasoline, gym memberships, cable TV and other utility bills, clothes shopping, and so on. We had none of those expenses during our sabbatical.

In fact, as we were closing up shop before our trip, it was sickening to slowly realize all the 'extra charges' we were paying monthly. These charges were hidden in our wireless bill, our cable bill, and almost every bill we had. Pulling the plug would end up being more financially responsible than I had thought.

✦ ADAM'S TRAVEL JOURNAL

There is no reliable Internet in many places around the world, so we've already been spending a little more quality time together in the evenings. We talk, drink wine and beer, and we maybe watch a bit of a movie.

PLANNING THE TRIP

When I first hatched the idea for the trip back in January of 2014, we began to casually brainstorm ideas and run some numbers. Then I got more serious and started to whiteboard it by February. Our first version of the trip was, "We'll go backpacking through Latin America. We'll go hiking through Asia." We wanted to stretch out our dollars as much as we could, in theory. Less developed places like Africa and Latin America are great opportunities to do that.

But then we realized that with four young children we should probably choose an easier and safer route. We figured we should have access to excellent healthcare, doctors, and good nutrition. Jessica and I could survive on a bottle of wine and a cheese plate; the kids not so much. "Let's keep things easier," we decided. We can take the family on a trip that is more exotic and ambitious when they're older. So ultimately, we stuck to places we knew intimately (Barcelona), had traveled through extensively (Australia), or where we knew we could at least maneuver the language (New Zealand).

Another goal of our trip was to reconnect with some people whom we hadn't seen in a while. As you read earlier, Jessica and I lived in Vancouver for three years. We wanted to reconnect with our friends there, and rekindle our love of that amazing city. So we started putting together a carefully planned itinerary with some of those goals in mind. It was no surprise that relationships were a key part of our trip. Seeing our friends and their growing families truly enriched our travels, and also provided many free places to stay! We started looking at dates. By March I was mapping out destinations, and by April we started booking flights and locking in dates and locations.

At the outset, my strategy was to book the major legs of our trip first. This is the route we took: Austin to Costa Rica, Costa Rica to Vancouver, Vancouver to San Francisco, San Francisco to San Diego, San Diego to

AROUND THE WORLD IN ONE YEAR

Hawaii, Hawaii to New Zealand, New Zealand to Australia, Australia to Thailand, Thailand to Spain, Spain to France, France to Italy, Italy to Greece, Greece to Germany, Germany to London, London to home. What I didn't do was book any accommodations or a lot of the shorter connecting flights. All of that we planned to handle on the road as it came up. The idea was to have an overall sense of where we wanted to go and for how long, but not to try to nail down every leg of a one-year itinerary in advance. In other words, we wanted to get our overall route booked, but leave plenty of room for flexibility.

Once we were on the road, planning became nearly a fulltime job. Jessica and I would probably spend twenty hours a week researching where we were going to stay next, figuring out schedules, researching transportation, negotiating prices and rates, and other logistics.

✎ ADAM'S TRAVEL JOURNAL

One sight I'll never forget is the strange wildlife that greeted us every time we arrived back at our rental in Nosara, Cost Rica. Giant crabs! The kids were mesmerized by these odd-looking creatures all over the back yard every day. I kept thinking to myself, "I wonder if they're edible?"

For a lot of people, waiting until the last minute to book flights or accommodations would be nerve-wracking. But one of the things I learned in my tour business is that some of the best deals are only available a few days—or even a few hours—in advance. During the Beijing Olympics, I booked hotels for my clients two years in advance, and the prices were pretty steep. But with my own family, I put us on a plane to China not knowing where we were going to stay on the day we arrived. That didn't stress me out at the time, and it didn't for this trip either. *We scored some of our deepest discounts and best deals by waiting until the last minute.* To repeat: suckers book early; you'll get the best deals by waiting until the last minute to secure your accommodations from homeowners.

I knew from my travel business that I would very likely be able to buy things for 30 cents on the dollar by waiting until the last minute. I didn't have a single accommodation booked the week before we left on our trip. For the first stop of our journey, Costa Rica, we found a place two or three nights before we left Austin. Available inventory can be had for a lower price a day or two before because the hotel owner or tour provider would rather get something than nothing. Unused inventory is like a bunch of bananas; eventually they just go rotten.

The trick is that you have to be willing to remain calm and accept uncertainty and the unknown. I didn't mind waiting until the last minute to book accommodations because I always knew that in a pinch I could whip out my credit card and book an expensive hotel. In contrast, most tourists want to book their vacations months in advance and have the peace of mind of knowing that everything is all set and locked in. *Peace of mind often comes at a premium of 40 to 60 percent.*

🖊 ADAM'S TRAVEL JOURNAL

```
For dinner, we had fried calamari, ceviche, focac-
cia, two pizzas (Jess ordered a second one), and Red
Snapper. Plus some beers, including Jungle Beer, a
Costa Rican craft beer. A typical dinner in Costa Rica.
```

FAMILY TEAMWORK

Part of the reason I wanted to go on this trip was to reconnect with Jessica. Before the sabbatical, I wouldn't say we weren't getting along, but it was a stressful time for us—especially after my big financial loss in London and in the aftermath of the Brazilian fiasco.

During our 15-year anniversary dinner, she actually started crying because of our difficult situation at the time. Here I was, at dinner, on the phone trying to spring my friends out of jail on our anniversary dinner. Not exactly romantic. I needed to reconnect with Jessica, bond with my children, and grow closer with my family as a whole. And I knew this year-long voyage would do just that.

✐ ADAM'S TRAVEL JOURNAL

```
I tried to sleep but couldn't. But I don't think
anything was in my head. It was not the usual anxiety
I have about money, career, time, etc. It was just
empty thoughts. It didn't bother me that I couldn't
sleep.
```

The trip gave us a chance to work as a team. We were going to be in it together, which was something that had always worked well for us in the past. Jessica and I have complementary skills; she's good at certain things I'm not good at, and vice versa. And we had plenty of experience running a business and traveling together. So I knew that whatever the challenges that we faced, we would be able to figure them out and grow closer in the process.

Travel at times can be a magnet for stress. You will encounter uncomfortable situations over and over again. But getting through these situations can unite people on so many levels.

And that's exactly how it ended up working out for us. We would very easily assign tasks, "You figure out what we should do tomorrow, I'll figure out how to get us there from the airport. You take Jett to the bathroom, I'll take Chiara to get something to eat, and we'll meet back here in 20." After a while this became almost a rhythm, a cadence that we relied on to help us multitask and get more done in less time. It felt like we could read each other's minds sometimes, and so the trip really did bring us together as a well-functioning team.

✏ ADAM'S TRAVEL JOURNAL

```
The monkeys in Costa Rica harassed us a few times,
which kind of freaked out Jessica. Eventually they
came down and grabbed a pack of Zane's baby food and
swiped it. I have four children and can honestly say
this was the first time that a monkey has stolen my
child's food! Well, the same thing happened shortly
thereafter with another snack. Apparently, Jessica
wasn't taking these monkeys seriously enough!
```

A BIG DECISION

From the start, Jessica was up for the trip. If she had any hesitation, it was that she thought I was going to ultimately back out, change *my* mind, and pull out the rug from under her. She would tell me, "This is a big stretch for someone who says he has a lot of anxiety about traveling." It was a fair comment. She was right, this really would be a stretch. But I believed it was a good idea to push myself outside of my comfort zone. Once she realized that I was not going to back out, she took the decision seriously, and so did I.

Most people are shocked that Jessica said yes so quickly. They sometimes ask what I would have done had she said no. The funny thing is that it never really occurred to me that she wouldn't be on board for a crazy adventure. I never saw convincing her as a possible obstacle to the trip. She loves travel and adventure as much as I do so I anticipated she'd jump at the chance.

THE NIGHT BEFORE OUR TRIP...

We dropped off the kids at Jess' parent's house. We had no idea when we would return to join them. During the day, we had considered delaying our trip by a couple days. Put simply, we were not ready. Bags weren't packed that well. House had a long way to go. By the time we returned to our home for the last time, it was 8:00 p.m. Our storage unit was closed for the night. My best friend Casey came over to help (and bring beer). "You guys aren't getting out of here anytime soon," he said. It pained us to hear it, but he was right. We were storing things in attic space and underneath staircases. We'd run out of boxes, so we started putting clothes in garbage bags and chucking them in the attic. At one point, at about 2:00 a.m., Jessica cried. It was a hard night, and as habitual procrastinators, we had a lot of work for the last night. At around 3:30 a.m. we drove to Jess's parents place, where our four children were peacefully sleeping. We would barely sleep an hour that night. We'd all wake up the next morning, none of us knowing what to really expect as we began this trip.

From my perspective, the trip made so much sense. I needed a break. I was fried. We needed to pause and press reset. And after all, we had all these frequent flier miles that, after years, felt like they were burning a hole in my pocket. What was the point of all that if not to take my family on an amazing trip? So I really don't know what I would have done if she said no. But she didn't.

With our friends and family, it was a bit of a tougher sell. Everyone was skeptical. You know how every family has one crazy family member - the black sheep who is a little wacky and lives in another state? I remember realizing one day when we were talking to family about the trip, "*We are* the crazy brother and sister!"

Friends and family in our inner circle knew that I was in pain. They knew that before Brazil. But to most people, selling your belongings, renting your house and running away from your problems didn't seem like a very adult thing to do.

Basically, people had one of two reactions. The first would be disbelief. "Are you *really* thinking about doing that?" And that reaction was understandable. After all, we had young children. We hadn't won the lottery. And it's not like we had anything booked other than tickets. Up until the very last minute we could have cancelled the whole thing, and it wouldn't really have cost us anything—just a few hundred bucks to put the miles back in our account.

For our closer friends and our family, the reaction was even more skeptical. "Is that really a good idea with everything that's been going on with you guys lately?" None of that skepticism bothered us much. We have always been the kind of people willing to take a sideways turn, to follow our hearts and do what our passion told us to. And I think our parents understood that. They didn't necessarily understand the trip, but they understood that we were the kind of people who did things differently.

✏ ADAM'S TRAVEL JOURNAL

```
It's Chiara's first time on a surfboard. She is so
light and athletic that she just pops up easily.
Within a few minute she rides a wave all the way to
shore. Within a few minutes after that, she's loving
it. She's a natural and she knows it. She rides waves
all the way in so far that her fin gets planted in
the sand. Go Chiara!
```

TRAVELING WITH CHILDREN

As I mentioned earlier, we have four children: Chiara, Jett, Blaise, and Zane. When we started the trip, our kids were ages 6, 4, 3, and 1. One of the big reasons we hesitated doing the sabbatical was my four-year-old son Jett. He has a sensory processing disorder and some social anxiety issues. But the net result is that he didn't travel well. He doesn't like transitions in general, whether it's a change in his schedule or diet or his daily routine—in other words, everything that would be thrown into disarray by traveling around the world. We knew this entire journey was going to make him uncomfortable. But we also believed it would be a growing experience for him.

✎ ADAM'S TRAVEL JOURNAL

```
I get home and notice the rear bumper has fallen off
the back of the rental van. Only in Costa Rica. I
jump back into the van and go looking for it with Jett
and Blaise. No luck finding the bumper. That's gonna
cost me since I declined the rental car insurance.
```

That's something Jessica and I talked a lot about. We asked ourselves, "Is it better to cater to someone's weaknesses or to their strengths?" And more than that, we love our son, but we're a family, and we don't believe that it's healthy to let everything revolve around one family member, whether it's our son or me or Jessica. We are a team and should act like a team.

Our oldest daughter was six and she was the only one who was officially in school. She had just finished kindergarten and was getting ready to start first grade. She also has a high level of emotional intelligence to couple her book smarts. So as part of her studies during the trip we had her keep a detailed journal. She wrote about 150 pages in it over the course of the sabbatical year. And some of her journal entries are pretty awesome. I'll include some of them in this book so you can get a feel for how a seven-year-old perceived our epic travels.

✏ ADAM'S TRAVEL JOURNAL

```
Grocery shopping was always an adventure. At one
grocery story in Arenal, Costa Rica, they had one of
those car-shaped shopping carts that the boys love be-
cause they're like driving a miniature vehicle. They
were pumped, and Blaise got to go first. Toward the
end, I made him get out. He threw a huge fit in the
store, kicking and screaming, and I think every
customer in that place looked at us. They had never
seen a crazy little redhead go ballistic in a grocery
store before, I'm guessing.
```

Chiara's also a voracious reader. When we talked to her teachers about the trip we asked them how we should keep her engaged intellectually while we were traveling. They basically said that since she likes reading so much, just keep her reading new books throughout the trip. So that became a big focus for us. Everywhere we went we did what we could to get her books. We also got an Amazon Kindle with an unlimited account so she could always have digital books to read. By the end of the trip we estimate that she read a couple hundred books.

Homeschooling was challenging for sure. It was mostly Jessica who did the heavy lifting with Chiara. Our daughter was an eager learner, but she pushed back on schoolwork. And at times, Jessica didn't have the patience to deal with Chiara during her many appeals to avoid schoolwork. Chiara enjoyed going to museums, learning about history trying new food and seeing sights and architecture. We always tried to find books that were associated with the places we were visiting. Sometimes that was hard, as in Thailand. In English-speaking places, like Australia, it was easier. We even got library cards when we visited New Zealand, Australia, and Vancouver. In order to do this, you will have to use a local address, and you might have to (slightly) stretch the truth on your length of residency. We would go the library and load up on whatever we could find that was relevant to the local culture and geography.

Towards the end of our trip, we would give Chiara the guidebook for wherever we were and have her plan one of our days. That was great. She would look on TripAdvisor.com and help pick a restaurant, which was fun for her, but a good exercise as well. Overall, after visiting countless museums and seeing places where world history actually happened, we believe the educational value of our trip far surpassed what our children would have learned in a preschool or a first grade classroom back in the States. Not to mention the lifetime worth of memories that our family will share and reminisce about for decades to come.

Probably the first question people ask is how we homeschooled our children. The struggles I witnessed with Jessica trying to teach Chiarawere legitimate. I believe it would be difficult to take a few hours every day to dedicate to typical 'schoolwork' with 3-4 children. But our children were listening to Italian, seeing Greek ruins and learning about Australian wildlife. I would argue this is more important than some of the busy work my kids come home with every day.

✏ ADAM'S TRAVEL JOURNAL

Tamarindo, Costa Rica

There was nothing extraordinary about this day. But it was a great day. One of my favorite days, actually, on this trip. Simple and fun. Swimming, good food/drink and an amazing family. This is what I love most about this trip.

GROWING CLOSER TO FAMILY

Each of my parents earned a Master's Degree in counseling, and my only sister is wrapping up her Master's now. So as a child growing up I was always talking about my feelings and my relationships, about what was inside. That definitely shapes how I act as a parent. Both Jessica and I try to communicate a lot with our kids, to hug them, and touch them, and talk with them—to try to build that closeness into the relationship.

But it's a lot of work. We had four rambunctious children under the age of seven at the beginning of this trip. And they're loud, they're physical, we laugh a lot, and wrestle a lot. We're like a walking tornado to be honest. When we're going through airports or to museums or some other public place, everyone is turning around to witness this spectacle of so many children with all that energy. We're all loud and outgoing so you can't help but notice us.

My kids are one of the primary reasons I wanted to take time off and go on the sabbatical. I wanted to do the trip was because I felt like I wasn't spending enough time with them. Fatherhood is the role that's the most important to me. And even though it was something I said (and felt), the truth was that during this moment of my life, I realized I wasn't living up to that value set. Before our trip I was only spending about two to three hours per day with them, which wasn't enough for me. As parents, our kids sleep 10+ hours a day and they're either at school or going back and forth for almost another 10 hours. That doesn't leave a lot of time for parents and intimacy. And how many of those few hours are we distracted? Looking at our phones? Watching TV?

Plus, Jett had those sensory issues and I wanted to understand that more—to understand *him* more. A lot of the worst episodes he had took place when I was traveling on business, when his world felt different—less stable and unstructured. Jessica would have to deal with it alone because I wasn't there. She would try to describe his painful episodes to me, but I didn't fully understand. Jett is a complicated kid, and I didn't get him. But I desperately wanted to, and I saw the trip as a chance to do that.

At the end of the day, I felt like I was working so hard on my business and it was creating a hole in my life. I didn't feel close with my children and Jessica. I felt embarrassed about not being happier and closer with them. I viewed this trip as a chance for me to get to know all my kids better, and for us to share bonding experiences and become closer as a family. And I needed this, especially for myself. It wasn't just about those little people.

When Jessica and I first started our business all of our friends would ask, "How could you be with your wife 24 hours a day?" Fair question, but the truth is I enjoyed every minute of it. We have always been unique in that way. I genuinely appreciated spending all that time with her during this magical year. Same with our kids. I loved being with them 24/7. When I look back on it, it does seem a little unusual; I basically spent 24 hours a day with them for a year. How extraordinary is that?

OMG! COSTA RICA OMG! MOMENT

We had plenty of OMG moments in Costa Rica. But spending a day at the thermal baths in Arenal was something we will never forget! This is basically a water park (called "The Springs") that has natural hot springs. There were probably 30 pools of varying temperatures throughout. There were slides, restaurants, shops, and swim up bars. And we had the entire resort to ourselves. It was our best day in Costa Rica and was truly an unforgettable ending to an amazing country.

LOL! COSTA RICA LOL! MOMENT

We were enjoying a sunny day in Arenal National Park in Costa Rica, and all of a sudden the storm clouds started to roll in... fast. It was about to downpour on all of us and the car was a mile away. Then the wind began to roar. But our son Blaise (age 3) refused to believe it was going to rain and ruin our day. He said, "It's not gonna rain!" Then it began to shower. Not wanting to leave, Blaise screamed, "It's not gonna rain!" not realizing he was getting soaked as he was saying this. Then it really started coming down. We all ran for the nearest shelter, which was the car, which was probably close to a mile away. Chiara enjoyed the rain. Jessica had Zane on her back in the baby carrier—he was sleeping until the rain came. After an exciting sprint back to the car, we were completely soaked. Blaise was still a little upset, even though I carried him the last few minutes. We got back to the room and we all had a good laugh about how fast the Costa Rican weather can change. We still give Blaise a hard time about, "It's not gonna rain." Note to self: bring rain gear or buy a cheap poncho (remember we're supposed to be traveling light!).

TRAVEL TIPS AND HACKS

iPads for the Kids!

The iPad is the single greatest tool for traveling with children. We bought a bunch of first and second generation iPads for the kids before we left. We picked them up cheap for about $75 each. And we loaded them up with games and books and cartoons. There is so much kids can do to occupy their minds on an iPad. And most of the games and content are designed to teach them motor skills, or reading skills, or other lessons. Before we had the iPads, the kids would moan and complain every time we took them on a long car ride. But with the iPads the complaining literally stopped completely. Now they look forward to long car rides and plane rides. The iPad is literally a game changer for traveling with kids.

The tricky part of giving kids iPads for travel is not becoming 'those parents.' You don't want to be sitting on the coast of Italy at dinner with your kids staring at their iPads. For us, these devices were solely used on 'travel' or 'transition' days, as we called them.

Charge Away

It's been mentioned various times, but use your credit cards. We probably spent less than $5,000 cash during the entire trip. Use various cards. Use cards like Capital One, Citibank, and US Bank that do not charge foreign transaction fees (3%). There are many cards that give back 2-5%. This is huge. Plus, if you pay $200 for a day cruise that is somehow canceled, you have insurance built in by being able to dispute that charge. AMEX isn't as universally accepted. Use a card that has car rental insurance covered as well. Review your checking account expenses to see what you're not spending on credit cards.

Music on the Road

Like most people, we have gone fully digital. For our music we use a blend of Spotify premium and Pandora. Most of the time, we have an internet connection. We have some music on our phone as well. It's important to invest in a portable Bluetooth speaker that can endure your trip. It doesn't need to be waterproof, but it needs to have good sound and be usable without AC power. Also important are several auxiliary cords. These come in handy not only with car rentals but also in homes where they actually have a great stereo system and all you need is the ability to plug in your phone. These cords are cheap and light weight, so I suggest getting a couple extra ones since you might lose them.

>   **Pro tip:** *Other essential cords include a splitter (so two kids can watch on one iPad) as well as a converter from your laptop to HDMI (so you can watch home movies where your 'home' happens to be). Kids*

headphones are also a good buy.

Booking Far in Advance

Note that cashing in frequent flier miles, especially for a family, is hard to do. If you're booking busy international routes, you'll want to book as early as possible. Typically, 330 days in advance is when the airlines will allow reservations, and if you're able to look that far ahead, I suggest that's when you redeem your mileage awards. This is especially true if you're booking 5-6 reward tickets like we were.

Sound Machines

When traveling to strange cities there is often a lot of noise outside the window at night. Traffic noise, sirens, loud voices, music, you name it. This can be unsettling for children (and adults). We found that traveling with a white noise sound generating machine can be very calming. After they get used to it, the sound machine even becomes a trigger that it's time for bed, and it puts them in the zone for sleep. There are even free apps for the iPad or iPhone that operate like a sound machine (white noise).

Eventually, as we tried throughout the trip to lighten our load, we ditched the sound machines, and solely used the iPad apps. Sound machines were not only good for a loud urban setting, but sometimes they were great for being in the middle of nowhere...when its too quiet!

Books for the children

It's difficult to homeschool kids (and keep them engaged) when you're traveling around the world. But it's easy to get them to read. Before we left on our trip we asked my oldest daughter's teacher for some advice. She said, "Just keep her reading. That's most important." Traveling requires hours and hours of down time, waiting in airports, train stations, bus stations, and time spent inside on rainy days. Having an ever-changing supply of books on hand for the kids is a great way to keep them learning and keep them occupied on long flights. Of course, buying books at retail prices gets to be ridiculously expensive, so we bought them from second hand bookstores, Salvation Army, or neighborhood markets. In fact, Goodwill (or the local equivalent thrift store) was typically our first stop when we're reach a new destination. Many places we stayed in that cater to families also have small libraries or book swaps. You simply donate a few books, and take a few new ones, so the library never runs out. This works with books for grown-ups, too.

"You have everything you need to build something far bigger than yourself."

—SETH GODIN

2. DON'T CREATE A SAFETY NET
Just Be Flexible

ONE OF THE THINGS I LOVE about travel is that you get outside your routine, get a fresh perspective, and gain experiences that are new and different. It puts your mind in a different place. It's a skill set, waking up in a strange city, or hearing a foreign language, or visiting some historical site that brings you in touch with the past. Or maybe it's a restaurant that offers you access to a different culture and their way of life. Whatever the reason, travel seems like a giant reset button. And believe me, I needed to press it.

The added benefit of getting outside of your routine is that travel gives you the opportunity to disconnect and to be distracted. You don't have any of the obligations of normal life—you can just go to a secluded beach somewhere and truly be in the moment. When it came to this trip, that idea really stood out for me. We could be totally focused on what was right in front of us, not be distracted by Facebook, email, business and all of the thousands of other things that pull us in different directions when we're wrestling with day-to-day "real life."

To make living in the moment possible, we continually tried to automate pieces of our life. In addition, we eliminated most of the stuff we had to deal with back home. I didn't have my business calling me every couple of days, for instance. This didn't happen overnight. But eventually, I was able to just focus on the next step of our trip—where we were going to stay, how we were going to get there, which restaurants we were going to eat at, what games my kids wanted to play, and relishing and enjoying every moment of it.

But to be in the moment and stay in the moment required us to do something that most people can't imagine: *live without a safety net.*

I mentioned earlier that right up until the week before our trip, it would have been easy to call the whole thing off and cancel the trip. Nobody would have blamed us. But that safety net disappeared once we actually began our journey. We structured things so that it would have been very difficult to quit and go back to our lives in the States. For example, a lot of our tickets were non-refundable once we began our travels. I had basically removed myself from the business; I didn't have a job and salary waiting back home. And perhaps most important, we had nothing to go back to, since we had rented out our home for the entire year.

Sound terrifying? For many people it would be. But for us it had the opposite effect. Our "no going back" attitude enabled us to stay fully engaged in the trip and fully committed to solving the inevitable problems that would arise. We weren't constantly asking ourselves, "Should we call it quits and just go home?" That's the problem with having a safety net—if you have one, you're probably going to use it. But we decided early on that we were all-in, and so there was very little internal conflict. The result was that we were able to totally disconnect from "real life" back home and completely immerse ourselves in our surroundings. Every experience was heightened. Every moment was felt and cherished.

To answer a question we are often asked, yes, of course there were tough moments where we considered not going the full year. But we had built the trip with various incentives throughout. The business class flight from Melbourne to Bangkok? I wasn't going to miss that. We looked forward to staying in Barcelona for most of the year, and we certainly couldn't retreat before that. And by the time we were rolling through Europe, we were having too much fun. But this trip will push you. It is not stress free, nor for the faint of heart.

✒ ADAM'S TRAVEL JOURNAL

People were not used to seeing families with four children in Costa Rica. So for the most part, they welcomed us. In fact, a guy was trying to sell us some little whistle type of toy (a little piece of art). We didn't really want it; I don't really buy much from street vendors. But he saw our kids and said he'd never seen an American family travel with four children. So he gave us one (no charge). We joked that you know you must have it bad when the street vendors feel sorry for you and are giving you stuff for free.

For us, that was a key lesson. When you venture out into the world, problems will inevitably happen, and you can either drive yourself crazy playing it safe and building in an escape hatch in case things get too tough. Or you can commit yourself to the process, keep moving forward, and make solving those problems part of the fun.

To be able to stay present, stay disconnected, and successfully navigate the trials and tribulations of a year-long trip around the world, it's important to remain flexible. You actually have to embrace uncertainty.

That means being comfortable with dealing with what's right in front of you rather than worrying about what's going to come up three weeks or three months from now. It starts with taking that blind leap of faith and jumping into your trip with no thoughts of going back on your decision.

Eventually, my set of problems became very simple: *where were our bags? Where were our children? Where were we staying tonight? Where were we going to eat?* That's it. Seriously.

In a certain sense, we built in a reverse safety net, if you will. We loved Europe, having spent so many years living there. So we included Europe toward the end of our itinerary. We knew that whatever else happened, our time in Europe would be incredible. Knowing we were going to end up in some of our favorite countries, I was hopeful that we wouldn't cut our trip short. Retreating home would be more challenging than continue traveling. Any time we struggled or got discouraged, we would say, "We're only a few months from being back in Spain."

✎ ADAM'S TRAVEL JOURNAL

It felt great to be back in Vancouver. I got lost on purpose driving around, remembering the one-way rules downtown. What an amazing city to live in and visit. I was so happy that we were spending a month here. We pointed out so many special places to Chiara, asking what she remembered. Not much…nothing, really (she wasn't even three years old when we moved away). We pointed out that this was *Jett's city*. I think he feels a small sense of pride and ownership since he was born here, which is cool. I ran out to get some beer, which although it was expensive, was also a cool experience after drinking almost nothing but Imperial lager for the last month in Costa Rica.

FLEXIBILITY RULES THE DAY

Our whole trip was built around flexibility. Flexibility gives you leverage, and gives you an advantage over the people you're competing with for accommodations. For instance, we were able to get cheaper regional flights because we could always leave a few days later or a few days earlier to take advantage of a lower fare. And when it came to accommodations, our only rule was that we had to have at least two rooms. But beyond that, we were willing to adapt. Sometimes that meant we would sleep with the baby in our room, or that all three boys had to sleep in the same room—sometimes even the same bed! But it was worth it. We saved a lot of money by being flexible.

Of course, flexibility can also lead to headaches and inconveniences. So you have to know going in that you'll be okay with not knowing exactly where you're going and where you're staying.

As we left Barcelona, we booked a really early morning trip to Granada. The flight was at 6:00 am so we had wake up at 4:00. It was pitch dark outside and Barcelona is a late night city, so there were actually more people out drinking than home sleeping at that hour. The taxi we called didn't show up (and Uber was outlawed in Spain). All the taxis were transporting drunks and partiers to and from bars and clubs. So I was running around looking for a ride, while Jessica tried to keep the kids from waking up the entire building standing inside the stairwell. Finally, I found a cab and we made it to the airport. We were late, but made it just in time to catch our flight. No big deal. We didn't panic. We didn't freak out. We remained flexible. I kept thinking that the worst case scenario, we'd miss the flight and get to go back to sleep (which I would have been okay with).

Yet our Granada adventure was just beginning. When we arrived, it was still pretty early in the morning. As we went to take a taxi to the airport, the driver turned us away. "Sorry, we can only take four people, not six," he said. We were in disbelief because our kids were tiny. And most Spanish aren't afraid to break a rule or two, especially in the south. We said, "No way are we paying for two taxis." So we ended up making a quick decision. I said, "I'll take the bags and three kids. Jess, you take the baby on the bus and we'll all meet at the hotel."

Jess and I were willing to split up if needed, or do whatever the situation called for, and just make those quick decisions without arguing. We knew that whatever problems we encountered would work themselves out. They always did. Including this time. Jessica's phone ran out of batteries on the bus ride to the hotel. Meanwhile, I ended up being dropped off at the wrong location. It was just a block away from our hotel, but I still had to lug all of the bags through the cobblestone streets along with all of the kids. (Note: did end up with one casualty—the wheel on one of our suitcases broke walking through those medieval streets. And a suitcase without a functioning wheel is worthless!) The point is this: yes, it was stressful, but it wasn't horrible. It was just one of those things you have to overcome when traveling. And once again, I promise you, the hard and crazy times are the ones you remember.

The key is to try to maintain a positive attitude when the shit hits the fan. We had four small children—six human beings—so we knew it wasn't realistic to try to plan our days with precision. We weren't going to commit to booking a 9:15 am sightseeing tour because we'd probably miss the bus. And we knew that sometimes our kids would have to skip a nap, which always sucked, but that's the way flexibility works. You have to adapt and make do. We would just put them to bed early that night. You have to embrace those tradeoffs and improvise. When everyone understands that flexibility is a key part of your game plan from day one, you may lose some security and structure, but you gain new adventures along the way.

Vancouver, British Columbia

`Blaise fell at the playground today and cut open the`
`scabs that he'd gotten at the airport just a couple`
`days before. Poor guy.`

THE TRIP BEGINS—PURA VIDA

Starting our trip in Costa Rica turned out to be a good decision. That country encapsulates what we wanted out of the trip. It had amazing culture, incredible beaches, good food, great people, and everything was pretty cheap. It was absolutely one of the highlights of the entire year.

I always joke that Costa Rica is like Latin American Disneyland. You get to see the locals, eat Latin American food and see it all authentically, just like a Costa Rican. But it's almost like a theme park. Most people speak English. The country relies on tourism, and safety isn't much of an issue. It's a beautiful playground. There's a ton of stuff to do. There is amazing wildlife everywhere. And the kids really loved it. You haven't lived until you've been woken up by monkeys. I remember those howler monkeys, I think they are the loudest mammals in the world. It was pretty extraordinary waking up to their shrieking and seeing them scale a papaya tree while we sipped our local morning coffee.

Costa Rica also marked a transition for me. I still felt broken for the first couple of weeks, and bummed out about my life in general. Costa Rica gave me the chance to disconnect from all that, and try to let go of the baggage I was still carrying around. In fact, I literally disconnected. This was the only place on the entire trip where I didn't have a phone. I didn't have a local SIM number so I just disconnected my America phone number. I still was checking email over WiFi and working on my computer, but there were many places where we didn't have Internet at all. So in Costa Rica I was able to really make a clean break and move away from the harried world

I left behind to embrace this new experience that was starting to unfold.

We stayed in Costa Rica for a month, and moved around a few times within the country—to four different areas (Manuel Antonio, Nosara, Playa Junquillal and Arenal). We stayed in some beautiful houses. The U.S. dollar stretched further there than anywhere else we went (except perhaps Thailand). It gave us the opportunity to do more and spend less. We could enjoy a delicious meal for the whole family for a fraction of the cost of a dinner out in Austin.

It also turned out that we arrived in August, which is off-season for Costa Rica. As a result, there weren't many other travelers around. We stayed in one complex that had a pool, and we were almost always the only ones in the water. The kids loved having the run of the place.

It rains a lot in August in Costa Rica. But that didn't stop us from doing anything—it just made things wet. It rained, stopped and we'd go back out! We did a lot of hiking, ziplining, surfing, ate some really good food, walked on the beach, played in the waves, and went swimming a lot.

One of my most vivid memories was the monkeys. We stayed at a place where we literally had monkeys in our backyard all the time. You can imagine how awesome this was for the kids. They felt like they each had their own personal monkey! Things can't get much cooler than that for a five-year-old. For me, it gave me the feeling of just being surrounded by nature. Half a year later, we'd have a similar experience with kangaroos running through our yard in Australia.

One of the rentals we had in the village of Nosara was particularly memorable. It took a while to get to—you had to drive an hour on a dirt road to reach this beautiful little village. It was so secluded there wasn't even a grocery store near us. It had a bohemian hippy vibe, filled with yoga camps, local surfers and plenty of expats. We basically had our own beach all to ourselves. We would swim every day, and the kids took surfing lessons nearby. To this day, our kids remember the three local restaurants in Playa Pelada, where we stayed: Olga's, La Luna and Il Pepperoni.

✍ ADAM'S TRAVEL JOURNAL

```
We met up with our old friends in Vancouver. It was
another late night that didn't see the kids get to bed
until almost 9:00 pm. But seeing, eating and drinking
with great friends—this is exactly what this part of
the trip was supposed to be about for us! So happy.
```

DO YOU SPEAK ENGLISH?

People sometimes ask me about dealing with language barriers when traveling. In Costa Rica, it wasn't a problem. Jessica and I had learned to speak Spanish in Barcelona (where we had spent three years of lives). I had taken Spanish in college, but I didn't realize I couldn't speak it until I got to Spain and could barely order off a menu. But as with all languages, when you use it every day you pick it up fast. I took all-day intensive Spanish language classes for months. When you *need* to learn something, it falls into place. This was another case where I was benefiting from not having a safety net.

But what if you don't know the language at all? For the most part, we picked countries where we could communicate effectively, one way or another. We decided on Spain, New Zealand, Australia, Canada, and Costa Rica for a reason. There were exceptions, though, such as when we visited Thailand. We spoke zero Thai. But I don't think it mattered. The language barrier sort of becomes part of the adventure. Knowing the language makes things easier, but one of the wonderful things about travel is being faced with uncomfortable situations. You have to problem solve and improvise. That's how you grow.

```
During naptime I went to Costco and ended up spend-
ing $400 on Doritos, licorice, olive oil, cheese and
other non-essentials. After naps, we walked outside
our back yard across the alley to a playground, where
we brought snacks, drinks and music. We ate a chicken
pot pie that I had picked up from Costco. Overall, we
felt pretty good about our first weekend in Vancouver.
Lots seen but so much more to see, do and experience.
Exciting times.
```

Logically, most people try to avoid discomfort. But I would argue that uncomfortable moments are not always bad. You may feel uneasy at the time you're going through them, but they'll end up being some of the best stories that you'll tell for the rest of your life. You won't be saying to your grandkids, "Let me tell you about the time we checked into our resort hotel without any problem and then went to the beach and relaxed without a care in the world." That's not interesting. Rather, you'll be saying, "Let me tell you about the time we got stuck in traffic behind a herd of goats, had to charter a rickety old fishing boat to get us to the island, and had our wallets stolen by pirates." Now that's interesting.

Besides, today you can download any number of apps that translate languages. Google and Apple maps are game changers when you're traveling abroad (*Tip: you can preload maps when you have wifi and then use the map when you're out in the country and don't have a cell signal*). Tools like this can be helpful when you're traveling, but you can't depend on them to get by. Because the Internet is spotty in most countries, especially mobile Internet, and inevitably at some point you're going to lose your phone or have a dead battery. And if you're not used to getting by on your own good judgment and keen travel skills instead of your iPhone, well, that can end in trouble. Not to mention, if you're staring at your phone all day you're robbing yourself of some of the sights and scenes—and isn't that the whole point of traveling?

OMG! VANCOUVER OMG! MOMENT

Honestly, it was really about the people here. We were able to spend a lot of time with some of our best friends in the world whom we knew from our time living in Vancouver. We ate at Blue Water Cafe, which is perhaps our favorite restaurant in the world and definitely the nicest 'date night' we had experienced during the trip. It was also the deepest sense of community that we built during the trip. All of the kids did classes at the local community center and made friends.

LOL! VANCOUVER LOL! MOMENT

Vancouver was the only time we 'lost' a kid. It wasn't a huge deal, but it was kind of funny. We had spent the evening with friends eating and drinking out in majestic Deep Cove. We got back late and unloaded the troops. By the time we opened up the front door, we realized that we had left Blaise in the car. Of course, we were only 30 feet away, but he was a little bit scared!

I would also add, from a parenting perspective, I think it's good for kids to see that Mom and Dad don't have everything all figured out. Children tend to see parents as omniscient. I think it's better that they realize how you don't actually have all the answers, and that you can improvise and adapt as needed. This doesn't mean you're helpless; rather, you problem solve and use your ingenuity.

You have to be comfortable figuring out where you're going, or reading a printed train schedule, or when the buses leave, or asking strangers for help when you're lost. Your kids know *they* don't have all the answers, and it's healthy for them to see that you don't either. This will be empowering for kids. So when your kid asks you when you're going to arrive, it's okay to say "I don't know" if you're lost in the middle of nowhere. "But we'll figure it out!" You don't want to freak 'em out, after all.

We made it a point not to *fear* discomfort on our trip. We had to accept that we'd hit a few bumps in the road—and sometimes big ones. If you don't know the language, so what? You'll get by. If your wallet gets stolen, you can get new credit cards. If your hotel cancels your reservation and you find yourself in a strange town with no place to stay, the trip just got that much more interesting. Consider it a blessing. You will figure it out!

✐ ADAM'S TRAVEL JOURNAL

Unfortunately, the Internet cuts in and out. If I were more organized and could actually write my book or do something productive I would consider the lack of online activity to be a good thing. But for now, I need to check email, plan our trip and do random other tasks.

KEEP YOUR OPTIONS OPEN

Other than our international flights, we would seldom plan our trip more than a week in advance. Some people might look at that level of unpredictability and panic. I get it. You're Type-A. You need a plan. *You need certainty.*

But the way we thought about it was that we were on a constant search for our next adventure. We never knew where we would end up and what was around the next corner. Keeping your options open is one of the smartest and most liberating ways to travel. It also allows you to change direction at a moment's notice and go wherever your whim takes you. If you're locked into a non-refundable hotel in one city, but you learn about an amazing local music festival happening a few hours away in a different city, you've got a tough choice to make. Better to keep the itinerary as open as possible so you can take advantage of unexpected opportunities as they pop up.

Planning what to see and do in between our long-haul flights was kind of our main job. Instead of pulling out my hair running my high-stress business back home, Jessica and I were having a blast as full-time adventure planners. We would look at guidebooks using Amazon unlimited and read about all the places we might like to visit.

Once we had some ideas on where we wanted to go, I would start hammering out thirty emails to different accommodations looking for deals. And usually finding them. Then we'd start figuring out how we were going to get there.

✎ ADAM'S TRAVEL JOURNAL

We woke up and headed out for breakfast. We knew we couldn't afford breakfast at the Westin Hotel, but they didn't give us much guidance on where to find a cheap diner either. So we wandered a bit until we found a Starbucks. We used points to buy coffee and breakfast sandwiches. We joked that we got the hotel free (using miles) as well as breakfast (using points) and that we were off to a good start in San Francisco, one of the most expensive cities in the country.

TRAVELING WITH CHILDREN

Chiara had mixed feelings at the start of the trip. She was enthusiastic a few months before we left, but as our departure date drew closer she began worrying about missing her friends, her extended family and her way of life. She said she didn't want to leave Austin. Understandable at her age. I could, of course, relate; I was feeling some of the same emotions.

The other kids liked travel, or what they had experienced of it up to that point. Two months before, we had spent two weeks as a family in Rio. But really they were so young they didn't understand what was going on—they had no clue what a year was, and they spent the first part of the trip struggling to figure out what we were doing. But they're kids, and all they really want to do is play. So for the younger ones, I think the transition was easier for them.

The kids loved being able to move to new houses. It was thrilling to arrive somewhere unique and pick out rooms. And if accommodations were too small or too noisy, there was something great about knowing that we'd be in a new place with new opportunities in the coming days. Our children began to appreciate our nomadic lifestyle in that way.

On the other hand, the little guys on routine. And parents thrive on a consistent sleep schedule. Well, talk about the need for flexibility. Every single place we stayed in Costa Rica ended up not having curtains on the windows. So we'd all end up waking up every morning at 5:00 a.m. (when the sun came up) to the sound of monkeys and birds chattering. Combine that with swimming all day in the sun, and everyone was taking long naps in the middle of the afternoon.

The travel days were hard on everyone. As mentioned earlier, one of our secret weapons was the iPad. Our children don't get to watch much TV at home, and don't ever really get to play on an iPad. By allowing them to play with their tablets on travel days, it actually made them *look forward* to long car and airplane trips. When we stayed 4-5 weeks in one place, we would add more structured time for school, workbooks and create more of a routine for everyone.

Before we came up with that genius idea it was always like, "Oh my gosh, we're going to be stuck in a car for *thirty minutes!*" With the trusty iPads, now the reaction was more like, "We're going to go on a five-hour bus ride? I can't wait to get on the bus!"

✎ ADAM'S TRAVEL JOURNAL

San Francisco

We took an Uber to Crystal's wedding and got there at 5:05 for the 5:00 wedding. We rushed in and ended up walking right past the wedding because we didn't recognize anyone, and everyone was really dressed up. We circled around the area for another 10 minutes. It was a small wedding, about forty people, and it was (drumroll, please….) black tie! I was wearing jeans, converse sneakers and a long sleeve button down shirt. My usual "work outfit" and the most casual I had ever dressed for a wedding in my life. The boys were equally casual with tennis shoes and long sleeve button down shirts and jeans. I was mortified. Eventually, I stopped being self-conscious about the fact that everyone was staring at me throughout the course of the night. I was able to borrow a black tie from a waiter. And a few gin and tonics didn't hurt.

ADAPTING TO LIFE ON THE ROAD

It took me a while to disconnect and really let go of all the business stress that occupied my days and nights back home. In part that was because it took the outside world a while to realize I had disconnected. I'd have vendors and business contacts emailing me, thinking I was still back at my office working full time. So I'd have to introduce them—via email—to their new point of contact. For months, people at work would still be cc'ing me on requests and asking questions. I'd reply, "In Costa Rica, can't help. Sorry!" But over time, those emails became less and less frequent as everyone figured out what we were doing. At some point during the course of the trip, I remember thinking maybe my email was broken (by how few messages that had come in overnight).

OMG! SAN FRANCISCO OMG! MOMENT

We were near the Market District in San Francisco and most of the kids were on the playground before we ran to the bathroom. I stood outside with Zane as Jessica went in the public bathroom with the three older kids. I heard yelling and screaming from inside the bathroom. I later told Jessica that it was like listening as my family was being murdered and I could hear their screams. Apparently, because there were a few of them in there, coming and going, somehow they had set off the self-cleaning action of the public bathroom. The entire bathroom completely soaked itself. Jett jumped on the wall and scaled it like Spiderman. Our daughter freaked out; even her socks were drenched, and she couldn't get over it. "This is one of those things you just can't control," Jessica told Chiara, "My feet are also soaked. But whining and complaining won't change anything."

Everyone has their own style and comfort level of "disconnectedness" when they go on vacation. Some people turn off the phone completely, others check it twenty times a day. I won't tell you what to do, but if you do an extended travel sabbatical, I know you will find a level that works for you and your family. In general, I believe you'll want to minimize how much management of your life back home you're dealing with while on sabbatical. Because too much of that will prevent you from being in the moment, and squeezing as much joy and rejuvenation out of your trip as you possibly can.

Over the course of weeks and months I would unsubscribe from email lists and e-newsletters. I even learned to build systems and processes for dealing with the "real world." Gradually I started to see the flood of emails slowing down to a trickle. I realized that you didn't have to respond to most emails right away. It was a process, but after two or three months I had gone from waking up to more than 100 emails in my in-box, to a point where practically no one was writing to me. I was so successful at disconnecting that I started to question my self-importance! While I'm being a little sarcastic here, I realized how much value I was putting into being 'busy.' As the trip progressed I slowly got to a place where it felt fantastic to be free of the rat race. And soon enough I actually stopped checking email daily. Imagine that if you can!

OMG! HAWAII OMG! MOMENT

Even though we had been to the Greek island of Santorini eight times in our life, we'd never actually visited Hawaii before. There were a few OMG moments here. Hawaii was special because this was us saying goodbye to the United States for a *long* time. So we mailed back packages, bought cheap stuff from TJ Maxx, and got ready to leave the good old USA. Tip: discount retailers like Ross, Wal-Mart, and the 99 Cent Store simply do not exist outside of the USA. Yes, buying cheap stuff is an American luxury, or excess.

We celebrated Chiara's 7th birthday at Duke's Restaurant. I remember that being a really special evening of blowing out seven candles with our feet in the sand. Celebrating everyone's birthday in a different place (Hawaii, Costa Rica, Santa Barbara, Italy, Munich and Australia) was overall a pretty unforgettable experience.

Unsubscribing from email lists is an easy place to start. Most of us are on a dozen different email lists. You might think, "Well, I'll just delete those emails without looking at them." But inevitably you're going to find yourself thinking, "Oh, this one looks interesting—let me just open it and skim it really quick." Or, "I'm gonna save this email and I'll read it later." And so it sits in your inbox and you end up seeing it six or seven times and it starts causing you anxiety until you eventually give up and think, "I'll just delete it." All of these very small decisions actually take up quite a bit of time and mental processing power. My advice, just unsubscribe from as much as possible. Or use a service like unroll.me. You can always re-subscribe later.

Another aspect of reducing inbound email is managing expectations of the people back home. In the modern world it can feel like every email requires a fast response. But the main reason people expect an instant response from us is because they're accustomed to receiving one. These days if you wait more than a day to respond to someone they'll usually email you again. And again. But if you start taking a few *days* to answer them, then *that's* what they'll come to accept. It'll be the new norm. So start responding after a few days have gone by, then gradually let your response time slip to a week or more. They'll get the picture. I promise.

Same goes for length of emails. If you always answer emails with a paragraph or two, they're going to think they have to write back a paragraph or two. You'd be surprised how effective a one or two word email can be.

✎ ADAM'S TRAVEL JOURNAL

This was our last day in Hawaii. We decided we wanted to get out and do some more, so we took the bus out to Hanauma Bay and snorkeled. We got out by 8:10 that morning and had to run in order to catch the bus. I was impressed that we made it. The bus ride took quite a while so I was glad that we got up early. I bought some masks and snorkels that morning at a corner store. I knew that Jett probably wouldn't like the feeling of a snorkel, but he insisted and I wanted to let him try it. Chiara loved the experience and I think she was in the water for the entire time we were there, almost four hours. She probably got a little dehydrated from the experience but kept wanting to go back and said it was one of the best days of her life. Any time a child says that to a parent, well, it warms your heart.

And here's the really funny thing. Most people who email you are not doing it because they actually *need* your input, but because they see emailing you as the most efficient way of dealing with an issue. For me, I would often ignore emails from employees. I would think, "You can figure it out. You don't need me to tell you where this red folder is—there aren't many places to look." People will become more self-reliant if you stop making it efficient for them to rely on you.

ADAM'S TRAVEL JOURNAL

We went down to New Zealand's famous Hot Water Beach at 8:45 after spending the morning packing. We dug around for half an hour trying to hit gold. The kids slowly started invading our neighbors large "hot tub" area. At first they pushed back, then finally they gave in and eventually asked all of us if we wanted to join. We did. We were cold and tired after tirelessly digging around in the sand all morning. And before too long they left, leaving us with a huge hot water area for our family. Unfortunately, the heat was pretty intense. We could barely sit in most spots. But it was such a unique and memorable experience we stayed as long as we could. After an hour or so, we finally headed back and showered. Amazing memories. But now, on to the next adventure.

You may also want to consider setting up an auto-away response that deliberately discourages more email. For example, your auto-away response could say something like, "Hello! As you may know, my family and I are in the middle of a 12-month around the world sabbatical. Needless to say, I will have limited access to email. So feel free to send me a *very* short email, but don't expect a response any time soon." That should help people get the picture.

KAIKOURA: ONCE IN A LIFETIME SWIM WITH DOLPHINS!

Kaikoura was a quiet, gray seaside town in New Zealand known for whale watching and dolphins. We decided to take Jett and Chiara to experience this bucket list swim. Once we got there, however, it was explained that logistically it wasn't going to work with one parent and two kids. So Jett, who was already reluctant, had to sit this one out. We took the boat out into the ocean until we found our first bevy of dolphins. As we sat on the back of the boat waiting to get in the water, Chiara started to cry. "Its so cold! I can't do it." Well, Daddy had already paid $100+ per person and we were here. Sorry, Chiara, I thought, as I pushed her into the water, which was freezing! Our feet and hands weren't covered and felt like they'd been dipped in ice. But we swam with dolphins! They weaved through us like we were playmates. After that initial shock, Chiara couldn't get the smile off her face. She also didn't mind the hot chocolate and cookies on the ride back at the end of it all.

Gradually you will adjust to your new, less-connected lifestyle. After spending most of your time connected by computers, cell phones, wifi, cable TV, apps, and even pizza delivery, it is a bit unsettling when you cut off all that communication and social interaction. But then something magical happens. You reconnect with yourself and your family in a whole new way. By giving up one thing, you gain something a thousand times more valuable. Your kids will forget your unhealthy obsession with starting at that small screen.

FAIRLIE UNFORGETTABLE

Ok, there are places you'll forget on your trip. And some you'll remember for strange reasons. In the middle of a long road trip, we stopped in a town called Fairlie. It didn't have much more than a restaurant and a grocery store, but as far as New Zealand goes, this was a kind of a big dot on the map. The owners of the place we rented had to bring over firewood to warm up the house. There were 30+ year old toys and dolls, which were kind of freaky. We had a couple pet sheep in the back. Chiara hated this house. She still moans about Fairlie being her least favorite place in the world! Ironically, she lost the first tooth of the trip in this house.

TRAVEL TIPS AND HACKS

VRBO vs. Airbnb

We used both sites extensively during our trip. In my opinion, and at that time, VRBO was made up mostly of properties owned by professionals. Owners were usually older, and at times, more ready to make a deal.

VRBO owners were renting their properties year-round as an income-producing business. Here's why that's important. VRBO owners seemed to be willing to negotiate and come down on price.

When we went to Paris, for example, we found that most of the property owners on Airbnb were just testing the waters by listing their house. They were in fact living there full-time, but if the right offer for for the right amount of time came along, they'd be willing to rent you their flat. I've had my personal home on Airbnb/VRBO for the last few years with this same intent, so I can hardly criticize.

Airbnb users are ultimately younger, and savvier. They know the market rates better. They're perhaps managing a large number of properties. They respond quicker. At times, the owners are actually budding entrepreneurs who have acquired the property with the intent of generating more cash as a vacation rental.

On both platforms, we definitely found people who were willing to wheel and deal. As I said, being able to negotiate was a big part of our cost-cutting strategy on the trip. And we got some really good deals. We averaged a little over $100 per night over the course of our journey. And we stayed in some pretty nice, often expensive, places.

We were able to pull this off simply because we would hit it hard. We were not shy about writing to dozens of people and asking for steep discounts. You'd be surprised how often it works.

I compared this business strategy to a few friends I had in college and how they approached girls. I knew some guys who would ask 100 girls to hook up during the course of a night out. When the first 99 say no, we would all make fun of the poor bastard for being rejected all night. Then the 100th girl would agree to go home with him and suddenly he's a genius.

My approach was similar. I would write to 25 or 35 properties. I would tell them about my family, my intentions, and my budget.

At times, I'd be writing a $350 per night place and requesting to book it for $100 a night. Most of them didn't respond. But if I was writing 30+ properties for a weekend in Rome—I didn't need them all to come down in price. I just needed one place, one owner, to recognize that taking my booking was better than having the place go empty.

Of course, this strategy is more effective when you wait until the last minute.

Food Costs

No matter what city you are in anywhere in the world, your food costs can vary widely. They mostly depend on how often you prepare your own meals vs. eat in restaurants, and what level or restaurant you prefer. Foodies who insist on gourmet meals every night will have triple or quadruple the food cost of travelers who cook their own meals. Street food and local markets are often a healthy, hearty, and inexpensive option. Breakfast is usually cereal or something simple at home before we begin the day. It's also important to consider which meals are important to you. We enjoyed eating out for dinner. But we ran into other families who liked sharing breakfast together. We typically didn't feel good (financially or health-wise) when we'd eat out three times a day.

Seek Out Local Events

You should always try to find fun local events in places you're visiting. Festivals were truly an amazing part of our trip, and we made it a point to seek out those opportunities. Some were pure luck (Thailand's water festival) and a few were more intentional (Auckland's Christmas Parade). You'll never go wrong by making the effort to attend local festivals and cultural events.

Pay for Internet and a Data Plan

Don't get too cheap about Internet. You can get amazing data plans for your prepaid cell phones. And most places on Airbnb and VRBO will include internet. I found that having a good Internet connection really helped us feel closer to 'home' at times when it was needed. There is nothing to cure a bout of being homesick like a Facetime call with the grandparents. Because we were spontaneously planning a majority of the trip, Internet was necessary to keep laying out the next leg. I wouldn't suggesting going more than a few days without internet. You might miss *something* important!

Don't Look Back

One thing that people have studied over the years is regret, and how that correlates to happiness. When you are planning this trip, keep your eyes on the present... and maybe the future a little, too. Don't go and look at your Facebook feed on Thanksgiving and get emotional that you're not in the USA. Don't second guess prices on tickets (that you already bought) by going back. If you're choosing between Vietnam and Thailand, make the decision and don't ever think about it again. Your sabbatical is a time for progress.

"When I was five years old, my mom always told me that happiness was the key to life. When I went to school, they asked me what I wanted to be when I grew up. I wrote down 'happy.' They told me I didn't understand the assignment, and I told them they didn't understand life."

—JOHN LENNON

3. HOW TO MAKE THE TRIP COMFORTABLE
(You Can't)

THERE ARE SOME PEOPLE whose ideal form of travel is finding that all-inclusive resort where they never have to worry about a thing. No problems to solve, no decisions to make, no risk of something going wrong. There's nothing wrong with that, but I would call that a vacation, not travel. And that's not what this book is about. Relaxing on the beach at an all-inclusive resort wasn't for us, anyway. Our dream was about maximizing the experience, absorbing the local culture, seeing the world, and doing it all for less money than we thought possible. If you can afford to spend a year flying from Four Seasons to Four Seasons, and that's what you want to do, more power to you. I'm sure that would be a pretty fun way to do it.

In my opinion, comfort is overrated. People stagnate in their careers because they're comfortable. A comfortable athlete is a contradiction in terms. If you want to grow, to do something special, to achieve any sort of happiness, my view is that you have to become comfortable being *un*comfortable.

I remember reading that Tim Ferris made his friends do an experiment. After ordering a coffee, you had to ask the barista if you could have a discount. Sounds easy, right? Try it. It will inevitably make you uncomfortable. And it's not about the discount. It's about the feeling, which is easy to trigger. But that feeling of being uncomfortable only lasts a few seconds.

💬 OMG! NEW ZEALAND OMG! MOMENT

We had a great time in Waiheke Island, where we had an amazing house for about $100 per night. Plus, we toured some great wineries there that had on-site playgrounds for the kids. For us, kid-friendly breweries and wineries were always locations we sought out! However, the highlight was probably our last week there, stopping in Wanaka (our favorite place up until that point) and then Queenstown, where we flew to Australia.

It was great getting ready for Christmas in New Zealand and starting Hanukkah there as well; our family celebrates both. We had an amazing place in Queenstown with a huge backyard shared by the whole hotel complex. We were housed next to the manager and our kids would play in the back yard together every evening. It was such a good way to end our experience in a magical country with friendly people. We booked the three-bedroom hotel apartment using miles, so it didn't cost us anything out of pocket.

💬 LOL! NEW ZEALAND LOL! MOMENT

We drove from Auckland to Queenstown (more than 2000 miles) and I got a flat tire on the way to dropping off the rental car at the very end of the trip, within two miles of the car rental place (99.9% of the way through our journey). I hadn't changed a tire in many years and the guys at the rental car office were 'out' in Queenstown. So I was told I had to either pay $300 or figure out how to change it myself. I was in the heart of Queenstown and had to pull over at a Holiday Inn parking lot and change the tire, calling the rental guys back in Auckland every few minutes for instructions since it had been so long since I'd changed a tire.

Travel is inherently uncomfortable. Its unpredictable. And that's a good thing! You're constantly putting yourself in strange new situations, and that means you have to deal with new challenges. All the hotels are booked, where are you going to sleep tonight? It just started pouring rain and you have no umbrellas. The train conductors are on strike. Everyone is tired and cranky and crying (and not just the kids!). The flights are sold out. These are just a few of the hundreds of travel dilemmas you will likely face in a year-long sabbatical trip around the world. But guess what, you will handle every situation.

The most uncomfortable parts of the trip usually involve dealing with other people. I've already mentioned that we have four loud and energetic kids. One time we found a note in our hotel room that said, "Letting your children scream indoors like wild beasts is incredibly inconsiderate. –Sincerely, Karma." Ouch!

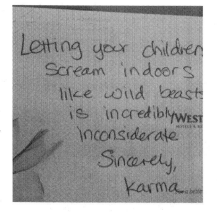

On one level, I was embarrassed by that note. But on another level, I was angry, both with my kids and with the anonymous note writer. What kind of gutless coward slips a note like this under someone's door? In situations like that you go through all sorts of emotions: embarrassment, shame, anger, frustration. We had a few interactions like that and they are never easy. But we never let it ruin our trip, or even our day.

We walked through the downtown area and stopped by the Christmas Parade in perfect timing to see Santa pull up on a fire truck. Chiara and Jett were perfectly positioned as he got out of the truck, but Jett froze up. He was frustrated afterward as he thought it could be his only chance to see Santa and tell him what he wanted for Christmas. I told him about Chiara and her trip to Disneyland and how she locked up meeting Sleeping Beauty. He felt better.

Another time, Jessica was having a moment with Zane (our one year old) in the middle of a piazza in Torino, Italy. And frankly he was being a pain in the ass. He was throwing a fit and rolling around on the filthy ground. This lady came up and started lecturing Jessica in Italian, "We don't let our kids roll around on the ground in Italy. Pick the child up." As you can imagine, Jessica felt judged. She was angry. She was frustrated. This will happen. So prepare yourself.

In another instance, we were able to use our frequent flier miles to fly first class from Australia to Thailand. We were looking forward to that flight for six months—to be able to actually enjoy some comfort during such a long flight. It ended up being a disaster. First of all, there was the fact that our 21-month-old Zane had to sit on our lap for 12 hours. But the worst part was that we had this horrible dragon lady sitting behind us,. Every time Zane would raise his voice or do something, she would kick the seat. At one point, she yelled out 'shut up!' I get it—the expectation is higher in first class—but that was just ridiculous. She could have just put on her noise canceling Bose headphones…like I had done! Every time Zane made any kind of movement we felt like crawling into a hole and hiding from the universe. So much for a calm, relaxing, first class flight. We should have slummed it back in coach with our people!

But that's what family travel is, it's leaving your comfort zone behind. If you want comfort, stay home and watch movies on the couch in the air conditioning. If you want to see the world and create memories and laughable stories that will last a lifetime, then get comfortable being uncomfortable. By going on a sabbatical you're basically signing up for a string of amazing experiences punctuated by plenty of tough times. I actually think that going through the difficult times makes the good times even better.

AMAZING FINDS

Sometimes great stuff just falls into your lap. As I was writing to various hotels and accommodations in Auckland, I wasn't having much luck. But somehow, I was referred to Mary. She had a place in Pt. Chevalier, at the tip of Auckland and right on the beach. She would be gone for 15 days, so didn't have much flexibility (she lived full time in the home). It was a former changing room/bath house. The tide would move almost 100 meters back and forth each day, twice a day. But it was an amazing place. Because we were flexible in working around Mary's schedule, we got the place for barely $100 a night. This was one of our best deals of the entire trip. Our kids still refer to *Mary's house*.

✎ ADAM'S TRAVEL JOURNAL

Christmas Day, December 25th. The kids woke up around 7:00 and were super excited that Santa had come. They got tons of presents from Santa and we were able to open lots of them with my parents watching on Facetime. It was a great morning and hopefully they won't forget their Sydney, Australia Christmas. After that, both Jessica and I went for a run. We ran to Bronte Beach and saw the entire place getting packed with people going to the beach for Christmas. How else would an Aussie spend Christmas Day?

CHIARA'S JOURNAL

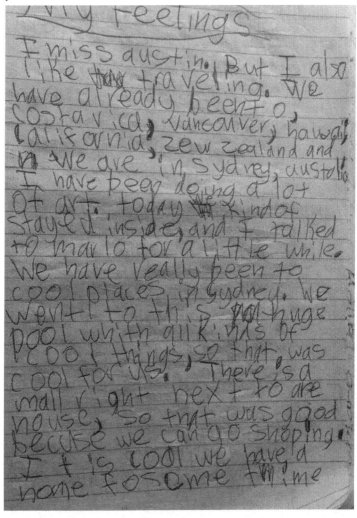

My feelings

I miss austin. But I also like traveling. We have already been to Costa rica, vancouver, hawaii, california, zew zealand and. We are in sydney, austalia. I have been doing a lot of art. today kind of stayed inside, and I talked to marlo for a little while. We have really been to cool places in sydney. We went to this not huge pool whith all kinds of cool things, so that was cool for us. There's a mall right next to are house, so that was good becuse we can go shoping. It is cool we have a none fosome time

In this journal entry, Chiara is describing how she
misses home, but also how much she loves Sydney. I
laughed out loud when she mentioned how cool it was
to be living next door to a shopping mall. Like mother
like daughter I guess.

SO GET COMFORTABLE BEING UNCOMFORTABLE

How do you get comfortable being uncomfortable? A big part of it comes
down to acceptance. That starts before the trip. Picture those moments
of getting lost, missing your flight, sleeping in a crowded train station or
a dirty hotel room, or even getting food poisoning. And then tell yourself,
"It's inevitable, and it's okay, we'll survive. It's all part of the travel experience." And you have to embrace the same attitude *during* the trip.

🖊 ADAM'S TRAVEL JOURNAL

As we wandered around Wellington, we were surprised
to like the city so much. We had heard about Auckland,
Queenstown, and Christchurch, but not so much about
the final stop on the North Island. We found Capital
E, which was a kid-themed museum. They had Christmas
decorations and our kids were able to work for a
while making baskets for children in need. Our kids
didn't totally understand how other kids wouldn't get
a visit from Santa. But once we explained what a lucky
position we were in, they started making these gifts
for kids with passion. It was an important lesson for
all of us, even the parents; be grateful. Give back.

Acceptance is really just the flip side of excitement. I remember reading that
Tony Robbins once cited all the human needs, with two of them being both

certainty as well as uncertainty. Think about that for a second. If you had total certainty, if you knew in advance "I'm going to do A, B, and C, and the result will be X, Y, and Z," there wouldn't be any excitement. Nobody wants that kind of certainty. Life would be like watching a movie you've already seen. No surprises. No suspense. No anticipation. Excitement means uncertainty, and to tolerate that you have to accept that sometimes things won't play out as you expect. And it's part of the fun.

OMG! SYDNEY OMG! MOMENT

Being able to have Santa visit us in Sydney was pretty cool. We stayed at Bondi Junction, right next to a huge mall, so we could do grocery shopping as well as Christmas shopping. The kids were so excited to celebrate Christmas there. They were also impressed by the two story LEGO Christmas tree. We shopped at K-Mart and Target. But oddly, both of these stores have no actual affiliation with their American counterparts (even though the logos are virtually the same). So it wasn't a huge surprise that the Target knockoff sold knockoff LEGOs.

LOL! SYDNEY LOL! MOMENT

Blaise locked himself in his own room one night by accidentally engaging the deadbolt on the door. And he couldn't figure out how to unlock it. He had to spend the night in the locked room while we figured out what to do. That was super frustrating because he was irrational and wouldn't listen to us trying to help him from the other side of the door. After spending the evening looking up door locks and posting on social media, I ended up just breaking down the door the next morning.

That's what travel is all about. It's about going into a zone where there is no script. You don't know how the next month or the next day or even the next hour will turn out. Travel helps us break those routines we get stuck in, often without realizing we're stuck. Some folks have the same sleep schedule, the same clothes, the same TV shows, the same meals, the same friends and social events. Does this sound familiar?

When you live in a cocoon of routine, you not only sentence yourself to boredom, but you start taking for granted the amazing things you do have. Want to appreciate something as simple as air conditioning? Vacation in South America during the summer where you're only escape is swimming and, if you're lucky, a ceiling fan.

OMG! AUSTRALIA OMG! MOMENT

We had a beautiful cabin in Hunter Valley, in wine country a couple hours outside outside of Sydney. There were dozens of kangaroos surrounding our place every day when we got back from wine tasting. The kids loved the kangaroos. As we adults would sit around the picnic table with a fire, the kids would run around hanging out with the 'roos.

LOL! AUSTRALIA LOL! MOMENT

Zane jumped off a small footbridge at the hotel in Noosa into the pool. He must have been under water for at least a few seconds. Did I mention Zane cannot swim?

Also, Australian immigration almost didn't let us out leave the country because we'd overstayed our visa by about ten days. Oops!

This was an especially important lesson for the kids. For example, I know they took their toys for granted. At home we had hundreds of toys, many that they never even played with. But on our sabbatical toys were scarce. So when they got a new one it was a really big deal. Americans are used to having what we want when we want it. Travel is a great way to reset our expectations of endless abundance, and learn to live with less… like most of the rest of the world.

Tolerating discomfort is a muscle that you can build. It's not a strong muscle at first, but it strengthens quickly. Athletes learn to lean in to the discomfort because they know that's where growth comes from. But it's not just for athletes, it's actually a universal truth.

✎ **ADAM'S TRAVEL JOURNAL**
SYDNEY, AUSTRALIA

```
On our last night, I BBQ'd my favorite lamb dish. It
was awesome. We also grilled everything that was left
in our fridge (all the veggies, crocodile sausages,
etc.). It was a fun night and we had tons to eat.
After that we went down to Bondi Beach. We walked
up and down Hall Street and got ice cream at Gelato
Messina. Then we went all the way to the beach and
had a jug of beer at the Bucket List. How fitting.
```

HOOKERS AND PIZZA

Travel is filled with the unexpected. Like hookers and pizza. You wouldn't think those two things would go together on a family vacation, but apparently the French disagree. We were visiting Paris and went to find this pizza place that TripAdvisor ranked very high. It turned out that the pizzeria was on a backstreet crowded with prostitutes. I'm talking a dozen or more hookers lining the street.

Now, it wasn't unsafe or anything. It was just filled with middle-aged prostitutes. I remember Chiara asking, "Mom, why do all the girls look so fancy around here?" Afterwards, I Googled the street name and found out that if you like 50-year-old prostitutes, that's the place to go in Paris! If you don't believe me, try searching "Rue Blondel Paris."

While we were inside getting our pizza, which was fantastic, my son accidentally knocked over a glass, which prompted us to realize it was probably time to leave. Jessica stayed behind to help clean up, while I walked out with the four kids. With our family, when it's time to leave a restaurant, it's time to leave a restaurant. But just at that moment there was a prostitute standing right there in the doorway, scouting for business. I thought, "This is awkward." On the one hand, I needed to wait for Jessica. But on the other hand, I didn't want to mess up her game; she's probably not going to make a lot of money with four young children standing next to her. So I decide, okay, let's start walking. Always better to keep the troops moving forward.

A couple minutes later, Jessica finally exited the pizzeria. I tried to motion for her but we were almost a block away at that point, and she started walking in the other direction. The French prostitute intervened and called out to Jessica, telling her that the guy with the four kids went the other way. Merci!

SPECIAL EVENTS ABROAD

Holidays
Spending Halloween in San Diego was really fun. Even though we are San Diego people, having a real community and being able to celebrate a real 'American' holiday in the USA was big.

Birthdays
We each had our birthdays in a unique place around the world. Each of the children still talks about this experience to this day, whether it was in Honolulu or Umbria.

Christmas and Hanukkah
I'm Jewish and Jessica is Catholic. Spending Hanukkah in Queenstown, New Zealand, then opening presents in Sydney, Australia, a few days later was pretty unforgettable.

Valentine's Day

We all wrote each other cards in Byron Bay, Australia, followed by a special Valentine's dinner that night.

Thanksgiving

We were in New Zealand where they have never heard of Thanksgiving, but that didn't stop us from celebrating with a big turkey and all the fixins.

Fourth of July

We celebrated America's Independence Day by organizing a barbecue in Greece. Their economy was melting down so it was a tense time.

YOU WON'T HAVE ALL THE ANSWERS

If you're traveling with young children, one of the lessons your kids will learn is that their parents don't have all the answers and can't magically solve every problem. We've all dealt with the frustration of a kid who wants to go to school in his favorite shirt every day, only to be told it's in the laundry so he can't wear it on that particular day. Well, travel inevitably leads to a lot of those types of situations. One of the really positive things that happens over time is that your kids learn to accept reality; they may not like something, but they begin to realize it is what it is.

OMG! THAILAND OMG! MOMENT

We had a hellacious day of traveling to arrive in Phuket. We rented a resort apartment, but it was off the beaten path. Because we'd flown, we got rid of most of our food and we had no cereal or snacks for breakfast the next morning. We woke up and the kids were starving. We wandered around and there was nothing nearby. I think it was a Sunday and many stores were closed. We found a lady who said she'd go to the store and get some groceries to cook for us, but we didn't want to wait for that.

We kept walking... then, there it was. Like a mirage, there was a Western looking resort hotel on the beach with hundreds of people eating a buffet breakfast outside on the veranda. We were thrilled. It cost about $12 per adult, and kids were free. This wasn't cheap for Thailand, but we'd have happily spent three times that amount in that moment. And it was great to have cappuccinos, pancakes, cereal and tons of other Western food. Since it was buffet style, let's just say we got our money's worth.

🗨 THAILAND LOL! MOMENT

Blaise ate so much at the Bangkok markets that he literally puked.

Whether it's a hotel room with no running water, or a plane that's stuck on the tarmac for hours, or a restaurant that doesn't have anything the kids want to eat. You're going to encounter these situations where you have to explain to your kids that there's something bad that you can't instantly solve, and that they're just going to have to accept it and make the best of it. But the amazing thing is that over time, they began to understand (even if they're young, like our children were). This is one of the most valuable life lessons anyone can learn, and I'm glad our children learned it so young.

Partly that's because we did our best to prepare them for the challenges of international travel. Take transition days for example, the days where we would be taking a long flight or driving for hours. We knew those days were going to be hard on the kids (and no picnic for us either). So we did our best to prep them on what to expect. We would explain what was going to happen, how long it was going to take, and how it would involve sitting still in a cramped space for a long time, waiting in lines, surrounded by grumpy strangers, and so on. We would also help them see why we were going through all that torture. We would explain where we were going, and all of the interesting and exciting things we would be seeing and doing there. Setting those expectations really helped the kids deal with the stress of traveling.

✎ ADAM'S TRAVEL JOURNAL

February 14th, Valentine's Day, Byron Bay, Australia. We woke up and Jess made pumpkin pancakes for everyone. She had the kids make Valentine's boxes a couple days ago and we filled them up with notes. Chiara was really into it. The boys got LEGO minifigures (which they refer to as 'Lego-men'), so they found it hard to focus on anything other than that. Very nice notes were written. Jess went out for a run and brought Chiara, who rode her bike with confidence. That was cool, and Chiara compares riding her bike to swimming, both things she now loves so much. Finding new and unique ways to celebrate holidays away from home is one of the joys of extended travel.

YOU CAN'T CONTROL THE UNCONTROLLABLE

Sometimes, though, no matter how much preparation you do, things still go awry. Greece was a place where we were dealing with challenge and uncertainty on a regular basis. We were there during the first week of July 2015. Greece's economy was spiraling downward and the country was about to take an important vote on whether to remain the European Union. Everyone was talking about this imminent economic meltdown, and wondering how bad it could get. We felt like we had flown into the eye of the storm.

Friends and family once again questioned our sanity by not altering our plans in order to avoid Greece during such a tense time. We tried our best to roll with it, but we were slightly nervous. We would go to the ATM each day and take out the maximum amount of cash, around 400 euros. We'd also pay with credit cards when possible, booking as much stuff in advance as we could, in case things went south. I wanted to stockpile as much cash as possible because the thought was in my mind, "You never know, I might need 3,000 Euros to get us all out of this country at some point." Thankfully the economic storm passed and we didn't have to enact our emergency plan.

OMG! *BARCELONA OMG! MOMENT*

Stepping into Sagrada Familia for the first time in almost fifteen years was pretty amazing. I also ran my first race in more than ten years in Barcelona and ended up winning the entire race (the Sagrada Familia 5 Miler). That was neat for the kids to be able to watch their dad win a race. It was also a significant milestone of how much healthier I had become as a result of this trip.

There was a great restaurant by our flat called La Paradeta where you select the food (fish/shellfish) and tell them how to cook it (fried/grilled, etc.). It's almost like fast food but overall a great experience that we all loved.

🗨 BARCELONA LOL! MOMENT

We sent the two little guys to school daily from 8:00-12:00. It was pretty hilarious that Blaise would go to school every day and never talk about it. We'd probe him and all he would say was 'Bon dia!' with a huge smile. That means good day in Catalan. That is a recurring joke in our family to this day. Bon dia!

SOME CONFLICT IS INEVITABLE

Our first day in the Greek islands was rough, however. We arrived in Paros via ferry, which took forever and left Jett—who, as I've mentioned, doesn't handle transitions well—feeling totally revved-up and out of control. So we got to our hotel, which was an amazing luxury resort. We were able to snag a $400 room for just $150 a night because we were flexible with our dates, and we filled in a hole in their inventory for them. It was gorgeous.

As the guy from the hotel is showing us around, my son just went nuts. He took off his shirt, jumped on the hot tub cover, and ran around like a caged animal. You have to keep in mind that we're a big family and for some reason that is always met with a bit of skepticism when we're booking accommodations. We had to sell ourselves by telling people, "Oh, we're an easy-going group, we'll take good care of your place." So you can imagine how embarrassing it was when I had just told the hotel clerk that line and then my son goes berserk. I just smiled and shrugged.

Let's face it, no matter how well your children behave, four kids are going to be hard on a hotel room. We did our best to take care of the places we stayed in, but there was inevitably some… shall we say… wear and tear. We broke a lamp here, scuffed the walls there, and we would just pay for any serious damage—no big deal. We rented out our home back in the States through AirBnB, and from our perspective, we understood that our tenants weren't going to leave the place in better condition than they found it. That's just how it goes.

Buying soccer jerseys for the family from Nigerians and them getting raided by the police a short time later was pretty funny, especially having to explain it to the kids. Fortunately, we got to keep our knock-off Barça jerseys.

But it turns out not everyone has the same easy-going philosophy. We were in Barcelona for two weeks, and the lady who owned the place ended up calling us out for leaving it dirty. Now, to be fair, she was right—it was dirty when we left—but it was also dirty when we got there. I mean it was honestly disgusting—dog hair everywhere, nasty filth under the couch so that when my kids would drop a toy down there and grab it they'd come out with a hand covered in dust, lint, and dog hair. It was definitely not a clean place, especially for kids, but I never complained. Again, my philosophy was just to accept that things won't always be perfect.

But then the landlord calls us out and says, "I can't believe how dirty your kids left it." I just couldn't let it slide. I said, "Okay, sorry, I have to unleash on you because the place was filthy when we got there. I didn't even feel comfortable there with my kids. It was the only negative review I left on Airbnb during our trip.

✎ *ADAM'S TRAVEL JOURNAL*

```
Today marks seven months of traveling. Wow. I know
we can make it. But it's tough at times.
```

Overall, we had great experiences using Airbnb and VRBO. Of course, there can be headaches. And it's important to understand expectations (regarding cleaning and other details). With most Airbnb places, they charge you a cleaning fee, which for us was a plus. Rather than be responsible for leaving the place in the same condition we found it, it was always better not having to worry about vacuuming and just paying the $30 fee instead. Packing up on departure day is stressful enough with a pack of children; having to vacuum and clean counters adds another level of work that you don't want to deal with.

✎ ADAM'S TRAVEL JOURNAL

This was our day to do the Eiffel Tower. We got there about 10:15 and there was already a sizeable line. We couldn't book tickets online for some reason. We were committed to wait, though, and the line was moving reasonably fast. It took about an hour to get tickets and actually go up, and we found it way too crowded every step of the way. Once we were up halfway, we had to wait in another line to go up all the way to the top where they were selling 12 euro glasses of champagne.

Near the end of our trip, we stayed at a lady's place in Munich and she did the cleaning herself. The next day, she was frantically writing us. "This was a brand new place and there was a smudge on the 450 Euro futon, so I'm going to charge you 450 Euros." No way was I going to agree to that. So she opened up a dispute on Airbnb, showing a picture of the smudge. My argument was that, (a) it's not new once it becomes an Airbnb rental; it was going to get dirty now or next time, so this was just normal wear and tear. And, (b) I'm not even convinced we were responsible for the smudge.

Thankfully, Airbnb ultimately sided with us. But those types of interactions are stressful. We don't like conflict. Incidents involving confrontation will, of course, stress you out a little!

 **FRANCE OMG! MOMENT**

We were able to connect with our friends Cameron and Kim in Paris. They had two daughters and invited Chiara to come with them to Disneyland Europe. That was a great experience for her. And she had two sleepovers with their girls in Paris—which ironically were her first ever sleepovers with friends.

Cameron and Kim, who are both pretty worldly, joked that Chiara was more street-smart than they were, and that she was giving them tips on taking the metro. Chiara also mentioned to us that it was nice to be able to take taxis (vs. public transportation) with Cameron and Kim and to order whatever she wanted off the menu. *Don't get used to it, Chiara!*

🗨️ *FRANCE LOL! MOMENT*

Racing through the Paris subway and catching a curb with the stroller and having the wheel completely break was funny. Scary but funny. We had to leave the broken stroller near a dumpster. For us, a stroller was a way to restrict and strap down Zane. We would also typically load it up like a homeless person, with plastic bags full of food and clothing hanging off the side.

MOVE FAST OR STAY LONGER?

During much of our trip we would pick a city and then stay in that one place for weeks at a time. It was easier to relax when we weren't constantly packing and unpacking. So the real challenge for us was from the end of May through August. We had ten weeks of travel throughout Europe planned, and we were never anywhere for more than a week. That was the hardest part of the trip, but it was also really rewarding. We saw so many amazing places, it was worth packing up the whole family and moving every few days. But sorting suitcases takes time (and brain processing power).

But it also required us to constantly lighten our load. We kept dumping stuff along the way as if we were an airplane needing to jettison heavy items before takeoff. And we went with whatever transportation seemed to make sense at the time—taking trains, renting cars, and flights occasionally. We were able to book a flight in advance from Rome to Athens, for example, for only $50 per person. But it was a non-refundable fare. That was a risk, but it turned out to be great investment because even if something changed, and we lost the $250, it was worth it.

We tell anyone planning a trip to Europe to take advantage of the trains when you can. They're relatively cheap, they're fun, and it's nice not having to go through security or check luggage. Probably the best thing about train travel is that you are typically traveling from city center to city center. It's better with kids because there's lots of space on the trains to move around. And you don't have to deal with the kids needing to get up to go to the bathroom at precisely the time when the flight attendant tells you to stay seated (which is what always seems to happen with my boys). Stuff can still go wrong on a train, of course.

OMG! *ITALY OMG! MOMENT*

Spending Blaise's 4th birthday in Umbria at a villa we had rented. We got a great deal on it, about 130 Euros per night for a majestic property. He was anticipating his birthday for months. He told everyone we were going to have a pool party with guacamole, which we did that evening. But for his birthday lunch, there was a nearby rustic restaurant that served a muti-course traditional Sunday meal, which is customary in Italy. We are talking a 3-4 hour experience. It cut right into nap time. But we just went with the flow because everyone was loving it. They brought probably ten or twelve different courses and I'm sure the adults polished off a couple bottles of wine. This was something we used to do a lot of in Italy when we had lived there a decade before, but we weren't able to show the kids that type of experience. It was amazing.

🔵 LOL! *ITALY LOL! MOMENT*

Jett dropped his huge gelato in Rome...in front of everyone. And he *freaked out!* Hysterically. The guys at the gelato place were trying to calm him down by telling him they'd give him another, but he was so bummed he wasn't even listening. Finally, it got through when they scooped him another and placed it in his hand. I guess I can relate; that gelato was good and I might cry if I had dropped mine! We still rib him about it, though.

BAD MOMENTS SOMETIMES MAKE THE BEST MEMORIES

One of our most uncomfortable moments was when we were in Santorini, a stunningly beautiful island in Greece. We went to this restaurant we had always loved called Nikolas. We'd probably gone there at least a dozen times over the years, and we knew the two brothers who ran it. So we were excited to bring the whole family to meet them.

In past years, the restaurant had a line out the door so we were careful to get there early. That wasn't hard since we typically eat at 5:00 or 6:00 instead of 9:00 or 10:00 like most people do in Europe. But when we arrived at the restaurant, it was almost empty—except for a few Japanese tourists. That was the first clue.

The second thing we noticed was that they had a printed menu. In the past, they used to write everything up on a chalkboard, which they basically had to do since everything would change on a day-to-day basis. They were quick to take our order shortly after we'd been seated. After we excitedly ordered Greek salad, saganaki and moussaka, the food was out 30 seconds later, which is a giant warning sign. I can't even make cereal that fast.

And sure enough, the food was mediocre at best. But the really disappointing thing was the service. They were rude. They kept giving us dirty looks, not listening to us, not being nice. I'll admit that my two-year-old, Zane, wasn't behaving very well—he kept getting up from his seat and walking around. Many restaurant owners found our family kind of cute. At one point, one of the staff members picked him up and told us, "You need to control your son." Finally, Jessica said, "Man, you guys are treating us so bad."

So the owner came over, and it was one of the two brothers that I remembered from over the years, with my first trip going back 15 years. I tell him, "We've been coming here for years…" but he cuts me off and says, "No. I've had 300,000 people here and you have never been here before. I don't remember you. You've never been here." I just looked at Jessica thinking, "That is the weirdest thing anyone's ever said." Then I looked at him and said, "Okay, you admit you've had 300,000 people, but you're saying you remember every one of them?" I was perplexed. I was annoyed.

It just got worse from there, with Jessica going off on the guy, and the staff telling us we were horrible parents. It was almost surreal—just a weird, awkward interaction—and it left us shaken for the night. This was supposed to have been a special dinner and yet we walked away thinking, "What a ruined memory."

Places change. People change. Roll with the punches, and avoid Nikolas the next time you visit Santorini!

OMG! GREECE OMG! MOMENT

I did the four-hour hike with Chiara and Jett from the town of Fira to Oia one afternoon in the midday heat. It was really beautiful and we all had a huge sense of accomplishment. The views of the Caldera were breathtaking. We stopped for drinks, lunch and ice cream along the route, and to re-apply sunscreen in the intense heat. Everyone was impressed these two little kids could cover a six-mile hike in the middle of the day!

🗨️ LOL! GREECE LOL! MOMENT

Somehow, I had gotten sick with a fever in Naxos. Jessica and Chiara went out for a date and I would have an easy night with the boys. Zane pooped on the side of the pool. I had to scramble to try to clean up without anyone seeing it and having a *Caddyshack* moment.

GET OUT THERE

Your trip will be what you make of it. That might sound like a platitude, but I mean it. You have to decide what you want your trip—and each element of your trip—to be like, and then actively work to make that happen.

Do you want to be active? How active? Do you want to avoid the heat? The cold? Do you want to drive? Or avoid having a car? Do you prefer mountains or beach? Can you make due with two bedrooms? Or do you need three? These are important kinds of questions you just need to consider. There is no wrong answer, but thinking through your ideal trip beforehand will help you plan it better.

When we went to big cities, our goal was to *get out and do things*; to make sure we were experiencing everything we could. Being in a place like Rome, for example, you're forced to get out and see as much as you can.

We had kids who needed naps every day in the middle of the day. Sometimes that meant we'd have to go back to the rental in the afternoon. But we didn't want that to become an excuse either, so every now and then we would just let the kids sleep in the stroller under a shady tree or at a cafe. We had to just make decisions, some of them difficult, and none of them perfect.

One of the things we thought a lot about was where to stay. We actually tended to shy away from places that were too comfortable or too nice—especially when we were in a city. The nicer the accommodations, the more you won't want to leave. I am not saying to book a hostel so you'll want to be out all day. And I'm also not suggesting that you don't splurge every now and then to find some cool digs. This trip will be like a rollercoaster, with ups and downs.

Now, in some cases we stayed in places where there wasn't much to see or do. Byron Bay, for instance, is this Bohemian little town in Australia where there simply isn't a lot to do. So we consciously chose to use our time there as an opportunity to relax, recharge our batteries, and take it slow for a month. For example, there was a yoga studio next door to where we were staying. Jessica probably did more yoga in that month than she had in the five previous years combined. Byron Bay was a trip highlight. There were no museums and very little sightseeing. But it was great to feel like a local, relax, swim, do some yoga and take the kids to circus class.

Another one of our priorities continued to be bonding with our children. So one of the things we did was set up date nights once or twice a week with one of them. Instead of taking the entire crew out to dinner, Jessica might take out Chiara for sushi, or maybe I'd go on a bike ride alone with Jett and get some ice cream on the way back. Chiara, in particular, craved our personal attention. Date nights gave us a chance to really connect with the kids in a more intimate one-on-one way.

TRAVEL TIPS AND HACKS

The Case for an Occasional Splurge

It pays to splurge when you're doing once in a lifetime experiences. We swam with dolphins. We ziplined in Costa Rica. We took surfing lessons. We bought an annual pass to Wet-n-Wild in Australia (knowing we'd only go twice). We went to a hot springs resort in Costa Rica. You can't put a dollar sign on these types of experiences. They will be what you'll remember forever. Work these things into your budget. They'll happen. And they're worth it.

Costs Vary Widely by Country and Region

Europe is one of the most expensive places to travel. Remember that you can significantly reduce the cost of your trip by strategically choosing which countries to visit. We spent a good portion of our time in Europe (which is about as expensive as it gets). If you choose certain Asian or South American countries, you can often travel for a fraction of the cost of Europe. But prices can change significantly due to currency fluctuations, so research this as close as possible to your departure date.

Kindle Unlimited

This was one of the greatest deals ever for long-term travel. We bought a Kindle and used the Kindle app on our various iPads. We got an unlimited account for endless book downloads. Jessica and I used this, as well as the kids. If you can, get the largest amount of memory you can on the Kindle so you never run out of space for more books. Just remember to charge the Kindle every night so the batteries don't run out on long flights.

Get a Postal Box for Mail

Since we rented out our house we had no choice but to get a P.O. box.

But looking back, this would be a good idea even if you don't rent out your house. And when I say get a postal box I do not necessarily mean a box at the United States Post Office. Many places offer postal boxes now, including the UPS Store, Mailboxes, Etc., and others. Using the UPS store is nice because you can call them and they'll check your mail for you. So if you're expecting something important they can be on the lookout for it. Plus, they will accept mail from any carrier, including FedEx, UPS, US Mail and others. An actual P.O. box at the post office may not accept FedEx or UPS. To make things easier, I suggest using the various services that will scan your mail for free, with just a nominal monthly charge. For example, Traveling Mailbox offers a service for around $19.95 that gives you a virtual mailbox; they'll open and scan a decent amount of mail for you. They'll also forward specific documents for a fee.

Insurance

Lots of people ask about insurance. Here is the low-down. Get the basics. There is travel insurance that covers you in case you have a medical emergency while traveling. Most great credit cards cover you as well. We opted for this route. We got lucky, having very few illnesses or accidents. Car insurance: same thing. We got an extra policy through AMEX that was $19.95 every time we rented a car using our AMEX. We didn't have to do anything. It covered us. We canceled our American insurance because the coverage sucked overseas anyway.

Get a Selfie Stick!

Trust me, it's a great idea. A selfie stick will save you hundreds of times from asking complete strangers to take your family photo. And a collapsible selfie stick weighs practically nothing. Your first one will eventually break or get lost, but it won't be hard to find a street vendor in Venice or Madrid selling you a replacement.

"*The greatest reward and luxury of travel is to be able to experience everyday things as if for the first time, to be in a position in which almost nothing is so familiar it is taken for granted.*"

—BILL BRYSON

4. WHAT WILL YOU GAIN FROM THE TRIP?
It Will Be Immeasurable

WHEN I TELL PEOPLE ABOUT OUR TRIP and they say it's not possible for them, I always reply, "Are you sure?" This makes them stop and ponder. I think it's easy to dismiss the idea as too unusual, or too extreme. Without any thought it's easy to quickly conclude, "I don't have the money for that," or, "I don't have the time for that." But when you really sit down and run some numbers, think creatively, brainstorm, stockpile frequent flier miles and hotel points in advance, and approach the idea with a can-do attitude, you might be surprised by what you find.

In fact, I think a trip like this is logical and possible for many families. Especially if you own your own home and you can rent it out while you're traveling. You may have to cut your expenses way back and save money for a year or two or three before you go. But with proper planning, I think most families can find a way to make a year-long sabbatical a reality.

I've decided that taking ferries is one of my favorite ways to travel. They're big, stable, have snack bars and restaurants on board, there's plenty of room for the kids to run around and play, and the views are stunning. We took ferries in New Zealand, the Greek Isles, and several other places. Jessica even found $300 on the New Zealand ferry!

When I give lectures someone in the audience always says, "I'd love to do this. But my daughter is in 7th grade, she can't leave her friends." The children are always too old, or too young, or too fragile, or too smart. Or, "I just started a new job," or, "I've been in my job too long, I can't leave." There is always a valid reason that the timing is wrong. There's always going to be a reason *not* to do it. The key is to decide a year or two in advance that you *are* going to do it, and then just start planning.

I have a friend who wants to take a sabbatical around the world with his daughters… in five years! That is too long from now! It's unrealistic. Yet if you plan to go in three months, you'll likely come up short. Ideally, give yourself 9-24 months to plan this trip.

Many worthwhile experiences in life aren't logical.

A around-the-world trip may not be a logical "next step" for a typical family in North America. In fact, it's downright unusual. But a trip like this is an opportunity to not only experience something unique and amazing and magical, but also to connect with your family in a deeper and more meaningful way that is simply hard to do in the day-to-day hustle and bustle of life. Spending that amount of quality time together, problem solving, team building, laughing until it hurts, collapsing exhausted into bed at the end of a day of sightseeing, meeting new people from other countries, hearing a dozen different languages, visiting the places where history actually happened…it's all priceless. Not to mention one of the biggest benefits and learning experiences was just having our family be together for 24 hours a day for a year. We learned so much about one another. We grew incredibly close. I don't think any of us will ever be the same.

And the trip actually gets re-lived over and over again long after you're back home. It's pretty incredible in terms of the volume of memories and stories that we retell and remember continually. Memories from the trip come up in conversation almost daily with the kids. "Our trip around the world" is a phrase we hear constantly. "I remember that time during our trip around the world…" They don't always remember the bits and pieces or the details, but they remember the stories. We also have thousands of photos to remind of us this amazing sabbatical. Our kids love watching the slideshows together; I imagine we'll continue doing them for years to come.

Because we were gone for an entire year, every single day marks the anniversary of a special part of our trip. During our weekly family meetings, we ask the kids if they know where we were last year on the trip on that particular day. Because Jessica basically kept her photo journal on Facebook, we're reminded daily where we happened to be several years ago.

💬 OMG! GERMANY OMG! MOMENT

We spent our last night in Germany with one of my best friends, Frank, who lived in Dusseldorf. We sat in the Alstadt (old town) and drank tons of beer after watching a Bundesliga (soccer) game. There were a lot of people out, including both of our families as well as our friends Wolfgang and Petra and their children. It was like a street party. Everyone was rowdy and having fun. The kids loved being able to shout and scream the team chants as loud as they could.

I reflected on how different it was to be with my friend Frank at this time, because he had seen me in dark times the year before.

Frank was with me in Brazil when all shit broke loose. He spent every evening with me in what was one of the lowest points of my life. But on this magical weekend he saw me brimming with energy and full of joy after the most amazing year of my life. I was grateful to have spent time with him in that happy moment.

GERMANY LOL! MOMENT

During that last night our boys kept singing German chants with the locals. They would scream "Hey hey" to get everyone started. They loved being able to scream like that and have adults think it was funny. Unusual behavior for ze Germans!

HOW OUR DAUGHTER CHANGED ON THE TRIP

Our oldest daughter was born in Barcelona almost seven years before we took our sabbatical. She also spent three years living in Vancouver, Canada. She had spent time in Germany, China and Brazil before we took our trip. So she'd traveled more by age eight than most people do in their entire lives. And even before the age of seven, she understood the history of many of the places we were seeing. She comprehended more than the younger children how incredibly special our sabbatical trip was. And even after the trip was over she's still benefiting from it. In school when the teacher is talking about ancient Rome and showing pictures of the Pantheon my daughter raises her hand and says, "It's so much bigger than it looks in pictures. I've been there."

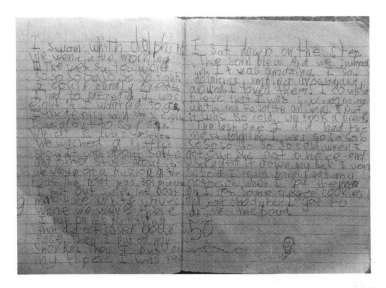

In this adorable journal entry, Chiara describes her experience swimming with the dolphins. When I read it I was cracking up because I had forgotten that children had to be at least eight years old to do it. She was only seven. So she journaled about how she told a little fib. It made me so happy to read in her own words how much she enjoyed the dolphin experience.

She knows more about real history than most kids because she's seen these places with her own eyes. It adds a perspective and a level of gut reaction that you simply cannot get from looking at pictures in a book. There is no better way to learn history than to combine reading about it with actually visiting the location and taking a tour. It helps solidify the lesson in the child's mind.

The trip also helped Chiara mature a lot. We put her in a lot of situations that were high-pressure at times. When you travel there are deadlines and things to remember and keep track of—especially with four young children. We relied on her a lot to help look after the little ones. Whether it was rushing to get all the bags all the bags onto the train before it left the station, or watching her younger brothers and keeping them wandering off, Chiara had to step up at times and be a leader. Chiara was also really good at asking questions and getting information, like what time the shuttle leaves or where we can get a taxi. She helped us grocery shop, decide on restaurants, and pick places to stay in.

Chiara even developed some leadership skills on the trip. There were so many decisions to on a daily basis, so we enlisted her help do research and asked for her opinion. We'd say, ask your brothers what they want to do and then make a decision and come back and tell us what you collectively want to do as a group. She was very involved in planning parts of the trip and deciding which excursions we should take. She'd read in her books about a historical event that happened nearby and she'd plan a detour so we could check it out. She continually contributed to our itinerary in a big way. Chiara also got interested in cooking. She made middle eastern soups, tzatziki, peanut butter protein balls, Greek salads, etc. We were very proud of her, and I could not imagine having done this trip without her.

Most of the time Chiara enjoyed contributing. But other times she just wanted to be a kid and be taken care of, so we let her do a lot of that, too. "Why do I have to do this? Why do I have to always help?" But then we'd say, "You get to decide what we do tomorrow. Here are your choices." She loved that. She, of course, enjoyed making key decisions more than the mundane tasks of taking her brother to the bathroom or buying groceries. But we relied on her a lot. We would develop various routines, like when boarding a train or checking out of our rental, and she was really good at wrangling the little ones and making sure that everything got done.

Chiara embraced that kind of responsibility and leadership because that fit well with her personality, and she got better at it as the year progressed.

PARENTING ABROAD

Some readers might suggest that what we were doing goes against typical Western parenting culture. Maybe it does. Jessica and I were raised in the United States and there are certain accepted and customary standards of parenting. But when you see the bigger world through travel, you relax and loosen up on some of those things. Our parenting style gradually changed as the trip went on.

For example, in the U.S. parents are opposed to leaving their kids alone on the playground and feel they have to always be on the lookout for creepers or pedophiles. Generally speaking, we of course try our best to avoid lowlifes and criminals.

And this is how Jessica and I were raised, too, with the idea if you leave your kids alone in the mall for 30 minutes they'll be kidnapped! But on a year-long around-the-world trip you gradually relax some of those long-held beliefs. The rest of the world isn't as scared as we are. We had to become comfortable not being able to keep our eyes on them at every moment. This was a conscious parenting decision. We don't think the world is out to get us; we choose not to believe that there is a predator around every corner. After extensive travel throughout the world we have come to believe that people are basically good and most places are a safe and welcoming environment for families and kids. I believe this perspective is important.

This philosophy was continually challenged. In Phuket, Thailand, we were staying in an upscale apartment hotel and we needed a babysitter. The guidebooks all recommended getting a babysitter through the building concierge. So we asked at the front desk and they told us babysitters cost $20 per hour. What?! In Thailand? That was way too expensive. So we negotiated, like we did on just about everything on this trip. Finally, they said they could get us a different babysitter for $10 per hour. That was still a lot in Thailand, but we agreed.

We figured out that this $10 per hour babysitter was probably a friend of someone *working* at the hotel, but not a babysitter *provided* by the hotel. When she showed up we quickly realized she spoke zero English. Hmmm. We began to worry a bit about leaving our kids with someone who spoke no English. *What if something happened?* What if one of the kids fell and needed medical attention? Would the babysitter even be able to call us and tell us?

So we improvised a solution. We gave Chiara an iPad and asked her to call us every half hour or so to check in. At this point, Chiara was pretty responsible and knew how to take care of the other kids. She knew what their bedtime was, how to get them ready for bed, get them to brush their teeth, how to turn on the sound machine, and so on. Jess and I decided to go to a restaurant close to the hotel, so we could hurry back if needed. And sure enough Chiara called us frequently, and every time my heart raced a little bit.

It was pretty funny because I guess we never told the kids that the babysitter doesn't speak English. So the whole time we were gone the kids were asking her questions and she would just nod. They thought she was just really shy and quiet. Finally, Chiara figured it out and told her siblings, "She's not shy, she just has no idea what we're saying."

In retrospect, should we have left our children with a total stranger who speaks no English in Thailand? Most parents would say no way. But these are the types of decisions you have to make when doing extended travel. It's a story I'm reluctant to share, but it's one I also think represents a lot of a (flexible) year abroad. *Babysitters will bring sanity.*

✎ ADAM'S TRAVEL JOURNAL

By sheer coincidence, we were in Thailand during one of the most bizarre but hilarious festivals I've ever seen. The Songkran Festival represents the Thai New Year. We called it the Water Fight Festival. As soon as the festival started we would be walking down the street and locals would run up to us and throw water on us. What?! The first time it happened we thought something was wrong. Then we looked around and realized that anyone and everyone was getting doused with water. Our kids loved it. At the end of the first day, someone gave us three huge super soakers. The kids were obsessed about walking through Bangkok with their machine guns filled with water. It was ironic that our entire three days in the Thai capital coincided with this special festival.

We had a similar experience in Italy. We hired a local babysitter to look after the kids so Jessica and I could have a date night. The babysitter spoke only a couple of words of English. Jessica and I both spoke Italian, so we were much more comfortable in this situation. At least the babysitter could call us and we'd be able to understand.

Honestly, the times we felt most in danger were simply driving in traffic. Especially in Bangkok. People, including children, get hit by cars and those reckless scooter drivers every day in Thailand. So we kept a close eye on the kids whenever we were crossing streets or near traffic. But we honestly never felt afraid that someone was going to kidnap or hurt our kids. It also helped that we deliberately chose lodging in neighborhoods that were considered safe. The guidebooks and online forums help a lot here. We were happy to pay a little more to be in a safer part of town. And we chose the countries we visited this way, too. For example, Costa Rica is considered the safest country in Latin America. We felt totally calm and at ease sitting in a sidewalk café while we watched our kids played in the playground across the street.

✏ ADAM'S TRAVEL JOURNAL

Running is a great way to multi-task, especially when traveling. I could do three things at once: see the sights, get in great physical condition, and listen to audiobooks on audible.com. So I ran almost every day to stay in shape. I put my earbuds in and listened to books while I ran. After a couple of months, I lost 20 pounds and was in the best shape I'd been in for nearly a decade. It felt wonderful. Jessica was also running more. When you go for a run you really get to notice the city, get a sense of the neighborhood you're in, and see life in a foreign country on a human scale. I knew running would help me stay in shape, but I never expected it to be such an enriching travel tool. Many times, during a run, I'd stumble upon a neighborhood, a café or bar that I'd be sure to remember and bring the family back to later. At the same time, I also would run down many dead end streets and boring areas. Better to do it alone on a run than carting around a bunch of kids.

ONE OF THE BIGGEST CHALLENGES: FEEDING EVERYONE

The biggest challenge, believe it or not, of traveling with children is feeding everyone. We tried it every way possible. We could eat in our apartment or Airbnb rental and cook the meal ourselves for 20 Euros. Or we could take the family out to a restaurant for 50 Euros. You can probably guess which of those options won out. By the time we went food shopping, came back to the room, washed and prepared the ingredients, had dinner, and cleaned up, it was a three-hour endeavor. And we were here to see the sights. We weren't there to do dishes and mop the floor for an hour every night. So nine times out of ten we ate out—especially for dinner.

Of course, there were exceptions:

- When we were at a place (Barcelona, Byron Bay, etc.) for a month or so, we'd have a real fridge with real food.
- When we were staying in places where the food quality didn't match up with the economics (e.g. Auckland)
- When we stayed in places where the food was just too expensive to justify eating out very much. In Vancouver, it was hard to go out for dinner with everyone for less than $100 CAD.

When you have four young children you have different criteria when it comes to selecting restaurants. Price and value were a consideration, of course. But even more important than that was, for lack of a better word, space. Many European restaurants are tiny and cramped. They shove as many tables and chairs into the place as they can. But with our big family we needed lots of room. The kids needed to move around, get up and down, walk outside, and so on. Plus, our kids are just loud. There are a bunch of them and they all have to be heard. We soon came to realize that most Europeans were not accustomed to the level of decibels that our family typically produced. So we'd actually scope out restaurants based on how much extra room there was, how wide the aisles were, what the acoustics were like, how many other costumers we were going to piss off, and if there was a place for the kids to play outside nearby the restaurant.

That's one of the things about extended travel that you simply don't get by taking a seven-day vacation. Or even a two-week vacation for that matter. You learn a lot about yourself, your family, and what is important to you in various situations. We figured out our restaurant criteria pretty quickly, and that served us well for the rest of the trip. We also figured out how to balance cost savings with convenience, because those two are often diametrically opposed.

During the trip, I looked at a journal I had kept in 2007 when just Jessica and I spent a few months traveling in Australia. It wasn't atypical to spend $100 AUD on dinner (with a couple nice appetizers and a good bottle of wine). I felt that it was ironic that eight years later, we were frequenting the same neighborhoods and spending less money—while feeding six people instead of just two!

✎ ADAM'S TRAVEL JOURNAL

At one point during the trip, in Byron Bay, Australia, Jessica bought a one-month yoga pass and she'd do a class about five times each week. And we enrolled the kids in all kinds of fun classes along the way, like circus school. They got to learn how to swing on the trapeze and all kinds of fun stuff.

ACCOMMODATIONS

We gradually learned that both convenience and time saving were very important when traveling with a large family. On the other hand, we also tried to save every penny we could. Part of saving money was just smiling and dialing, to use sales terminology, to find places that had extra inventory and would be willing to negotiate. We would often call or email twenty or thirty different rental properties or hotels to find the best deal. This was time well spent if we were planning to stay there for a week or more. But for one or two nights we didn't try so hard to get a lower price. We didn't have much leverage. Think about it, if you can negotiate a 20 Euro discount per night, and you're planning to stay for two weeks, that's a lot of money.

🌩️ UNFORGETTABLE MEMORY

Riding in wooden longboats through the floating markets in Thailand was such a unique experience. So many fascinating sights... and smells. We also visited exquisite temples that phots just don't do justice. You have to see them with your own eyes.

We also knew that the rest of the world is not like the United States where people live in giant 4,000 square foot homes with rooms upon rooms. Most of the rest of the world lives in a fraction of the space that we are used to. So we recalibrated our sense of space pretty quickly. Jessica and I actually preferred renting small places with tight quarters so that the family would be incentivized to get out and see the country. I'd always felt that European culture is built around getting outside and walking around. So renting smaller places with less room worked to our advantage—we would save money and we'd motivate the kids to get outside. Plus, the smaller places were quicker and easier to clean, which saved us time. We just knew that if we rented a large place with big screen TVs far from the attractions then we'd be more likely to relax and stay inside.

LOCATION, LOCATION, LOCATION

Our other driving philosophy regarding accommodations was location. We were willing to pay more to be in the thick of things. We wanted to maximize our experience so we wanted to be able to walk right outside our door and be in the most happening areas of a city. Gathering up the kids to take a 30-minute bus ride into the town just to save a few bucks on lodging was not what we wanted to do. But that might work well for someone else, especially if your kids are older or teenagers. Or if you just feel like you need more space.

Again, this is your trip. Make it about you. Our little ones were a challenge, and we valued being able to walk to a bunch of restaurants, to the grocery store, to parks, and any other attractions we were interested in. So we were willing to pay a premium to stay in the center of town. Or to keep costs down we'd lower our standards to stay downtown. We all agreed that we'd rather stay in a two-star hotel downtown than stay in a five-star hotel a 30-minute bus ride away. And generally speaking, we didn't have a car. This is an important piece of the puzzle to consider for yourself.

✐ ADAM'S TRAVEL JOURNAL

Dusseldorf, Germany

I can't believe this adventure is over. It has become 'normal life.' The trip was strange in that I was constantly having fun, while constantly looking forward to the next step. I enjoyed the planning, the negotiating for places, and encountering special people along the way.

AVOID WINTER, PACK LIGHT

Another lesson we learned when traveling with children was to avoid cold climates. If you plan your trip so that it's always sunny and warm where you are then you can pack much less in the way of clothing. T-shirts, shorts, and sandals don't take up much room. If you travel to cold places or mountains you'll need to bring boots, sweaters, thick socks, jackets, hats, scarves, mittens, gloves, and so on. And doing laundry will become cumbersome. When traveling with children take the amount of winter clothing you need and multiply it times five. And all those socks, gloves, hats, and boots mean you now have 30 more things to keep track of, pack, and replace if they get lost. For this reason, we decided to plan our trip to avoid places where we'd need snow boots and hats. Jessica and I would always refer to our trip as *Endless Summer.*

When you go on an around-the-world trip for a year there are plenty of days that you spend in transit—on planes, ferries, trains, buses, or long drives. We noticed that even a 5-hour train ride would affect the kids and wipe them out for the day. So one of the ways we tried to minimize the hassle of travel days was to try to get it over all at once, to just rip off the BandAid. In other words, we'd try to get all the way from our lodging in one city to our lodging in another city, doorstep to doorstep, in one day. We found this was better than breaking it up into two or three days of less intense travel. After all, if a six-hour day of travel was going to wipe out our kids, why do that two days in a row?

HUSBAND AND WIFE

This year-long adventure had a profound effect on the relationship between Jessica and me. She and I bonded early in our relationship through travel and living abroad. But due to the pressures and stress of my tour business and our ever growing family, I had sort of lost that love of travel that I once had. Travel was something that always united us. In the end, this trip brought us together and bonded us more closely than ever. When you share something of this magnitude with a spouse it really does deepen and solidify your bond. As Mark Twain famously wrote, "I have found out that there ain't no surer way to find out whether you like people or hate them than to travel with them."

UNFORGETTABLE MEMORY
We took the children to see a fascinating Bavarian dancing demonstration in Garmisch-Partenkirchen, Germany. They didn't quite know what to make of it, but I think they loved it.

If you're going to do this with a spouse, you have to balance the teamwork component with romance. The teamwork element comes naturally. You and your spouse will learn to work together to solve problems, make decisions, and deal with mini-disasters along the way. This usually means dividing and conquering based upon each of your strengths. Jessica and I have different skills and different things we're good at. For example, I was the one who would smile and dial thirty hotels and rentals and negotiate the best rates. She was better with putting kids down for naps and solving their problems. We divided up the duties. "Alright, we're going to Paris, I'm going to find the place to stay, you're going to plan the first couple days' excursions." Or "I'm going to figure out how to get from the train station to the rental, and you'll look up a restaurant for tonight." Together there was nothing that ever came up that we could not handle as a team. It was this constant interaction that was fun and rewarding because we both enjoyed the teamwork and executing the trip on a daily basis.

> **Note:** *traveling will test you and your spouse. More than once, we were both so frustrated we had to go our separate ways (taking a kid or two each, of course) to get some space. This is normal. You are spending every waking moment with your family. Things won't be perfect!*

But you have to make time for romance during all the teamwork and problem solving. We made it a point to get babysitters so we could have our date nights. Romance with your spouse in foreign countries is one of the most fun parts of extended travel. And you and your spouse can do things on date night that you can't do with the kids—going to clubs or bars or rock concerts or cabarets or cocktail parties. It really rekindled the passion we had for traveling together and experiencing different cultures. Not to mention, we could finally have some adult conversation after having spent every waking moment of the day surrounded by children.

The trip also deepened our relationship because it was sort of a nostalgia trip for us. We had been to or even lived in a lot of these cities earlier in our marriage. We had gone on our honeymoon to Barcelona, for example.

We had moved to Barcelona on two occasions (from 2000-2002 and 2007-2008) and the city was full of memories and friendships. We had very similar experiences connecting with people and places in Torino, Paris, Athens and Dusseldorf.

"I don't know where I'm going from here, but I promise it won't be boring."
—DAVID BOWIE

Another thing that helped me deepen my relationship with Jessica was a concept I wrote about earlier. When you spend a year traveling all of your problems and experiences are right there in front of you, in the moment. The joy of seeing the Eiffel Tower lit up at night takes total precedence over thoughts and anxieties about the future. Back in the States, when I would be out to dinner with my family, half the time my thoughts would be a million miles away—thinking about my business, calls I had to make, deals I had to close, weighing risks, and so on. But when you're on an epic adventure you gradually leave those worries behind and think only about what's right in front of you. You are forced to.

After a few months away from home those worries and thoughts that used to occupy your mind simply melt away. You have more pressing issues to deal with and decisions to make. "Where should we go next? Can the kids eat spicy Indian food? Did you pack the Dramamine?" This allows you to live in the moment—which is exactly what your family wants you to do. Be with them. Enjoy their company. Thrill at the awe of seeing the greatest sights on the planet with them. Laugh at dinner. Stay up past their bedtime one night to swing by the gelato place. I think its these moments that define your trip, maybe even your life.

 **UNFORGETTABLE MEMORY**

In Australia the kids were thrilled to wake up to see kangaroos in front of the cabin.

MISHAPS WILL HAPPEN

In fact, while we were on our sabbatical, my company back home basically imploded. The company I poured so much of my time and money into over twelve years hit a serious rough patch, and it looked like it was going under. If there was ever a point that I considered cutting our trip short and heading home, it happened on December 1st, barely four months into our trip. I received an email from my former partner. He informed me that I wouldn't be getting paid that day, or ever again. I was out.

I was frustrated. I was mad. I was embarrassed. But after assessing the situation I realized there wasn't much I could do to help or to solve the problems. I feared that if we ended our trip and went home there wouldn't be a company to come home to anyway.

I finally felt like I was starting to be in a good place mentally, a place of being able to disconnect and be happy where I was. I knew it wouldn't be a healthy thing for me to go back to fixing problems and trying to fix someone else's mistakes. So we powered on. No safety net. Remember?

Eventually I realized that all I had to worry about was my family and what was in the bags we were carrying. Everything else back home would take care of itself. After a couple of months on the road I stopped worrying about the stuff we put in storage in the U.S., about the people renting our house, about my business, whom I should hire when I get back, and all the thousands of petty worries and decisions that occupy most of our thoughts living back home.

Many people have said to us, "Oh a 12-month trip around the world sounds so stressful." But the exact opposite is true. What's stressful is the rat race that we all accept when living in the United States. The pressure to keep up with the neighbors, to succeed, to build a career or grow a business, and so on. On the road those things become less important. And you soon realize that the only thing that really matters is your family. This moment. Right now. If you have a deep interest in trying to live more in the present, you need to think about doing a trip like this.

SEIZE EACH MOMENT ALONG THE WAY

Another important lesson I learned—although it took me until the end of the trip to understand it—is that you should always take advantage of the moment and visit places the first time you see them. Let me explain. Throughout our trip we would be passing by a funky cool store or a historical site, and instead of stopping right then to check it out we would say, "That place is cool. We will come back another day." Well guess what? Another day never comes. We would get so busy with excursions and doing other things we would never make it back.

 **UNFORGETTABLE MEMORY**

In Seville, Spain we saw an unforgettable Flamenco dance show. We sought out cultural activities like this whenever possible.

My strong advice is to build in extra time as you're traveling around a city, leave an hour early, leave some extra time so you can stop and experience things that pop up along the way every day. If your tour bus leaves at 10:00 am, and it takes an hour to get there from your hotel, leave your hotel at 8:00 am instead of 9:00 am. That way you will have plenty of extra time to pop in to that exotic farmers market, or photograph that neighborhood garden, or stop and listen to that street performer. We missed out on a lot of cool sights and experiences by running late and saying, "We'll come back to this later."

A great example of this is our trip to see the Pantheon in Rome. We were hurrying to get the kids fed—it was way past their dinner time and they were starving—when we walked right by the Pantheon. My first instinct was, "We'll come back and see this tomorrow." But by the time we made it to Rome, I had learned the lesson from the paragraph above. I said, "Stop everyone. We're here. We're going inside the Pantheon. We may never get back here." Everyone grumbled at first. But once we got inside we were all mesmerized. The Pantheon was truly incredible. We only could stay a few minutes, and the visit was not perfect. But we did it, and travel is not about perfection. It's a great memory. Had we just walked by and said, "We'll come back tomorrow," I doubt we ever would have seen it.

While we were there, I snapped a picture of the whole family at the Pantheon—with my selfie stick (yeah, I'll own that one). Technically, it is not a very good picture—it's blurry, not composed very well, and a little out of focus. But it's symbolic of this important lesson: better to have a great memory of an imperfect visit to an important attraction, than to plan and hope for a perfect memory that never actually happens. And get this, even though that picture was not done very well it is one of the most liked and asked about photos from our entire trip. When I give lectures and keynote speeches about the sabbatical, this is one of the slides that generates the most attention.

UNFORGETTABLE MEMORY

In Phuket, Thailand we got to ride an elephant. Such an incredible, gentle giant. I wish we could have one for a family pet.

SPLURGE OCCASIONALLY

Another great way to create lasting memories on a trip like this is to occasionally splurge on something that would normally be way out of your budget. As I have said, we were pretty conscientious about always trying to lower our costs and negotiate lower rates on just about everything. But once in a while we would spend big on something that we really wanted. And often these were some of our best memories. I have a picture of Jessica and me on a beautiful rooftop bar in Bangkok. We decided to splurge on this expensive, luxury meal high above the city. We even took the kids to this place—but they're not in the picture because the lovely Thai waitresses were playing with the kids in another part of the club. In Bangkok we were used to spending maybe $30 for a nice dinner. This meal was four times that much. It was way out of our budget. But it was worth every penny. And it's still one of our favorite memories.

So definitely splurge once in a while. I think it's a necessary part of any extended trip—or even any vacation for that matter. Nice restaurants, luxury hotels, spa days, massages, expensive champagne at a rooftop club, amusement parks, or even the occasional first class flight. Each of these can be a splurge that results in amazing memories, not to mention a happier family and satisfied spouse. If you can use miles to bridge this gap, even better.

How do you afford the occasional splurge but still stay within your budget for the trip? Build occasional splurges into your trip budget. Or keep a separate credit card just for splurges. Surprise your spouse. "Honey, I booked us a suite at the Four Seasons tomorrow night. Just for one night, but it will be amazing." It's likely she won't hold this against you.

 **UNFORGETTABLE MEMORY**

Ringing in the New Year by watching the world famous fireworks in Sydney was surreal because I had seen it on TV practically my whole life. Watching in person was unforgettable.

LOOK FOR CONNECTIONS

One of the things we did before we left on our trip was to reach out to anyone and everyone we knew who either lived abroad, or knew someone who did. Then we'd tell them we're coming in to town, or we'd ask for an email introduction. It's amazing how this simple tactic led to some of our most memorable experiences. I have learned that most people love to welcome visitors and friends of friends, and show them a good time in their city.

A great example of this happened to us in Whistler, British Columbia, outside of Vancouver. My friend Ben ran a high-end destination management company whose specialty was taking care of VIPs during their ski trips to Whistler. Ben and I had done about $300k worth of business during the Winter Olympics and I considered him a friend. He knew all the best places. We told him we were coming to town and he hooked us up with this amazing, off-the-charts mountain chalet that was probably one of the nicest places we've ever stayed in. He basically hooked us up with the place for free --we only had to pay a cleaning service to clean it after we left. It was so nice I was worried that the kids might break a $100 plate that we'd be on for!

I have a photograph in my slideshow that I use at speeches from that house. It's a four story tall totem pole that runs up through the center of the chalet. It's so big the homebuilder literally had to use a helicopter to lift it into place. After we left, I wrote down the address and Googled the property. The chalet cost $6 million. So through reaching out to old friends and making connections before our trip we were able stay basically for free in a $6 million mountain chalet.

We had similar encounters with old friends along the way whom we hadn't seen in years. Many of them were Facebook friends, or maybe we'd get an end-of-year letter from them recapping the past year. So we were always in touch with them digitally. But sharing photos over the Internet pales in comparison to being able to sit down and share a meal with them face to face. Meeting old friends again in person after years apart is one of the great pleasures of travel, and of life in general. We actually planned our itinerary specifically to meet up with our old friends in several cities. This is a great way to really organize your itinerary. Go out of your way if it means connecting with someone.

LONGER STAYS EQUALS MORE CONNECTIONS

One of the great benefits of extended travel is having the luxury of staying longer in one place. When you stay in one place for a while you can get involved in more activities. For example, you can take immersive language classes, the kids can sign up for summer camps or children's classes, and they can even make friends. And when you're staying in the same neighborhood for a while you can get to know the neighbors, and even get invited over for dinner. In most countries we found that people are curious to talk with Americans, if for no other reason than to practice their English. In contrast, if you're just moving from place to place every couple of days or even every week you simply won't have time to make friends or get involved in the community. We found great recreation centers around the world that had classes and camps for the kids.

UNFORGETTABLE MEMORY

Ziplining in Costa Rica was really scary and totally thrilling. If you add Costa Rica to your sabbatical, ziplining is an absolute must. Don't miss it.

EXPECT MAGIC TO HAPPEN

I guarantee that throughout your sabbatical you will experience many magical moments. In fact, it's impossible not to. But you will increase the number of magical moments you encounter by following the advice in this book: remain flexible, be comfortable with being uncomfortable, splurge occasionally, etc. Go with the flow. You'll be dead in 100 years.

One of our most magical encounters happened in Italy. We had the whole family crammed into a tiny European minivan which was no bigger than a Honda Civic (even though it was somehow technically a minivan). We drove into this Italian beach town Viareggio. I knew nothing about the town, but it seemed like a place that was going to be overrun with tourists in a couple weeks. More importantly, it was a stopping point in between Torino and our next home in Tuscany. We arrived at our house; there was no place to park, so a man directed us to pull into a long driveway. The owner, Bruna, had four children of her own. She said she felt sorry for us, figuring that most people wouldn't want a last minute family to roll in, especially for such a short stay.

She said, in Italian, "You can stay in our guest house, but I forgot to tell you that we are having an event here tonight. A big art exhibit type of thing. I hope that doesn't bother you." We said, "Not at all." Well it turns out she totally under-sold the event. It was an amazing party with live music, art and sculpture, close to 100 people, food and drinks, and a fabulous atmosphere. Our children were running around playing with a half dozen little Italian kids. The music was playing. Jessica and I were sipping bold local Italian wines. It was one of those magical moments in life that I will always remember. I thought, "This is unforgettable. This is the magic of travel right here."

Call it serendipity. The reason that magical night happened is that we were adventurous, we took a chance, we were flexible, we hadn't planned every detail, and we were open to new experiences. But it was also an accident. It was luck. Allow yourself to get lucky. If we had locked in to an itinerary that was set in stone and we never deviated from it this would never have happened. If I would have extensively researched Viareggio, it's likely I would have found its online presence to be unremarkable.

The one-of-a-kind experiences you get during extended travel are some of the best reasons to take a year-long sabbatical. Because those experiences will become priceless memories. If I had it to do all over again, I might change a few little things along the way. I might spend more time in one place, and less time in another. But one thing that I would never change, is our decision to take a big risk and go on this amazing adventure. We feel so lucky and blessed to have had this opportunity to see the world with our children.

In fact, we are already talking about our next around-the-world adventure. Now that the kids are older, it will be easier and they'll remember it more. To be honest, if I have my way, year-long sabbaticals will become part of our lifestyle—maybe we'll do one every three years or so. Your children are only young once.

So we strongly encourage other families to seriously consider taking a similar trip. The benefits and memories will truly last a lifetime. If this book has inspired you, if the idea of a great family voyage intrigues you, but if you think taking a year-long sabbatical is impossible for you and your family, I have one question for you.

"Are you sure?"

TRAVEL TIPS AND HACKS

Social Media

My wife decided before the trip that she wanted to use Facebook to chronicle our journey. She realized that this was tricky. We didn't want to appear like we were bragging the entire trip. But Jessica wanted Facebook to operate as her journal. She put photos and thoughtful pieces of writing into posts almost daily. Sometimes they were long. "This is for me," she kept reminding herself. With Facebook memories, we are literally reminded every day where we were on this trip a year or two ago. I took a slightly different approach. I de-friended about 250 people (and was left with about 160 Facebook friends). I didn't want the judgement. People who didn't know my story didn't really understand the context of my trip. And I didn't feel the need to explain it all to acquaintances (vs. friends).

There is no wrong or right approach here. But it's a conversation you'll want to have before your trip. We printed a Facebook book after our trip that has the posts, photos and comments. It's a really fun way to go through our trip.

Social media is also a great way to connect with people. "What should be do with 48 hours in Seattle?" is truly a great question that can be answered through your social network. We accidentally discovered friends that were in Paris, Hawaii, and New Zealand during our trip. Without social media, we'd have missed these amazing opportunities.

Traveling Things

While we purposely dropped clothing and other items throughout our trip in order to lighten our load, the curious thing about travel is that what you don't end up deliberately getting rid of along the way stays in your luggage! There was the bag of licorice that made it from Vancouver to Hawaii to Australia to Thailand. There was the dried Catalan sausage that lasted almost three months until we finally got rid of it at our final stop in Greece. There were tiny kid trinkets that were carried from place to place, simply because they didn't take up make space. My advice, every couple of weeks, spend a little time weeding out the stuff you don't need. It will lighten your load, and give you fewer things to worry about. And tossing out things feels cleansing.

Gear for Kids

Traveling with young children definitely require bringing along some gear, some of which is actually required by law. We used BumbleBum inflatable booster seats, travel dining chairs, kids travel cots, an umbrella stroller, and more. For a complete list of our recommended travel gear please visit the website www. KeepMovingFast.com for links and recommendations.

Souvenirs

Your goal is absolutely to travel light. But that doesn't mean you can't get souvenirs and mementos to remember the trip. Whether it's a piece of art or just some driftwood from a memorable beach you enjoyed, pick up these things. But don't carry them the rest of the journey; ship them home. We sent parcels back to the USA throughout the course of our trip. We even sent a box from Australia to Spain (with jackets, etc.) realizing we didn't want to mule it around for the next four months. Send them as cheaply as possible because you're in no rush. And don't declare any value on the box since you're shipping mostly personal items. Other great souvenirs are shirts for the kids. They will always remember that $5 Paris pirate t-shirt we bought.

> **Tip:** *the exception for longevity in terms of souvenirs will be Thailand (and Asia in general). Stuff you buy isn't built to last long.*

Thrift Stores and Salvation Army

Children require a lot of stuff. They lose things like socks and hats along the way. Actually, it was remarkable to me how often one of our children would lose a shoe! FYI, one half of a pair of shoes is worthless. So we often found ourselves needing to shop for kids clothing, toys, and other items. We figured out that Goodwill and the Salvation Army have thrift stores all over the world, especially in the English speaking countries. This was a great hack for us. And the prices were pennies on the dollar compared to retail. In fact, we spent three and a half months in Australia and just kept filling our van with stuff at the end. On our way to the airport to leave, we stopped at Salvation Army and donated more than six boxes of stuff. That certainly lightened our load for the trip!

Hair Cuts

We traveled with four boys, so getting haircuts was an expense that could quickly add up. I started out with a set of clippers. I fried them in New Zealand (rookie mistake) so bought a cheap set there. Then we bought our last pair of European clippers in Barcelona, which we left in Greece at the end of the trip. I cut my own hair as well as my boys. Three pairs of hair clippers for less than $100 is a lot cheaper than getting haircuts for the family every month.

"What doesn't kill you only makes your book longer."

—ANTHONY KIEDIS

Conclusion
BACK HOME

TOWARD THE END OF OUR JOURNEY I think we all had a lot of intense emotions. I felt nostalgic about the trip and all the incredible memories we made. And Jessica and I were very proud of what we had accomplished. We set out to do a year around the world and we did it. There were times when we could have cut the trip short and come home. But we completed our journey as we planned. We did it! So there were feelings of great pride. And it felt good. What a beautiful experience.

But there was also sadness. Almost a feeling of loss as the trip was coming to an end.

On our penultimate night of the trip we were in Germany. We had dinner with an old friend of mine, and as I was walking home I started getting choked-up and teary-eyed. I thought, "Man, this is really over. We're flying home tomorrow." After a year of seeing the greatest sights the world has to offer it was now time to go back to the real world. "Time to re-join the rat race," I thought. And, I'm not gonna lie, it was a bit depressing. I had spent a year figuring out myself, disconnecting with a lot and re-connecting with a lot.

So the lesson here is to be prepared for a bumpy re-entry. It was especially hard on me for two reasons. First, the trip was so magical I never wanted it to end. And second, I spent so much time planning for the trip, I totally forgot to plan for *returning* from the trip. So if you do a sabbatical, be prepared emotionally and logistically for it to end. In the final month or two of your trip it's time to start preparing yourself mentally for re-entry back into normal life. If I had done that I think it would have been easier on me.

A NOTE ABOUT YOUR EVOLUTION

You will change. You will evolve. Your outlook on life, time, work, and vacation could be turned upside down. But keep in mind, your friends and family back home will not go through this change with you. They might even experience feelings of resentment and jealousy. You are, after all, having the experience of a lifetime. Your evolution (or possibly even revolution) might be hard for others to relate to.

ASSIMILATING BACK INTO EVERY DAY LIFE

Just as it takes a few months to adjust to a life of constant international travel, so too does it take some time to adjust to "normal life" back home upon your return. Regular life was, and honestly continues to be, a pretty big adjustment. Oddly enough, I think it's actually harder on the adults than on the children. Kids are so resilient and high energy, they leapt back into normal life seemingly without much trouble. Our oldest daughter was looking forward to starting school and making new friends. Our son who was in preschool when we left kind of forgot what it was like. He seemed to not know what to expect when we told him he was going back to school. But he adjusted fine. School equals structure, so kids fall right into it pretty quickly.

One of the hardest parts of getting back to normal was all of the admin. We joked a lot about the endless admin of life in the U.S. Paperwork, applications, utility bills, car registration, and so on. It seemed endless at times. I remember buying envelopes. Envelopes! We hadn't purchased or even used an envelope in what seemed like forever. But now we needed them daily for mailing bills, sending checks, applications, registrations, etc. The endless admin of normal life. These are the types of things we had been able to forget about.

CHILDREN GROW AND CHANGE

Blaise
As a result of our trip, my middle son, Blaise, truly came into his own in terms of being an extroverted, outgoing kid. Blaise would go up to strangers all the time and talk, learning words in whatever country we happened to be in. Because the trip was full of interactions with friends, both old and new, Blaise also grew attached quickly. "What's their names?" he would ask several times, only to sadly say "I'm gonna miss 'dem" a few moments later.

Being in a big family has its own challenges (everyone is vying for attention). Blaise definitely grew as a person. And he is still our most extroverted kid.

Zane
Our youngest child started the trip out as a baby. He couldn't walk. He couldn't talk. He traveled for free. He became blonde in Australia. He celebrated his second birthday in Munich,

Germany. Needless to say, he won't remember one thing from the trip. But we hope that he learned flexibility. He didn't get attached to things or places. He heard different languages and experienced a variation of weather, people and environments. I think these experiences at such a young age will only help him as he gets older.

Since we sold most of our furniture before we left on the trip, we now had to buy a home full of new stuff. Sounds like fun, but it was also a ton of work. As I write this our master bedroom has the king mattress and box spring sitting on the floor without a bed frame. Buying everything we needed to get a household with four children up and running again was harder than we had anticipated.

We didn't plan on the transition because we didn't really know what to expect. Before the trip we had done a ton of research and planning *for* the trip. But we planned practically nothing for our return. We didn't really have a strategy. We had, after all, been Austin residents when we left for Costa Rica. And 12 months later, we were returning to live in San Diego.

So a big piece of advice for long-term travelers is to think through your assimilation back into society and back into the routine of life back home. It really does take some thought.

If you rent out your house while you're taking a year sabbatical, the easiest move would probably be to rent it fully furnished. You can always negotiate on a few items that the renters may or may not want in the house, then you can move a few things around, put them in storage, or sell them off. But being able to return home and move right back into your house would be ideal. This is a huge advantage. Unfortunately, we didn't do it that way. In addition to living arrangements, we also had to figure out where to send the kids to school. What kind of car to buy. And a thousand other small decisions that had to be made basically all at the same time.

Adding to my frustration was the place I found myself in professionally.

As I mentioned in the last chapter, I was on the outside of the the business I spent more than a decade building. So I was starting from scratch.

I had planned to do a lot of work on my laptop during the sabbatical, but I could just never find the time. As you have read in these pages, this trip actually takes a lot of work! You won't have as much free time as you might have planned on.

This was especially true toward the end of the journey when we were in Europe. At that point we were never in one place for long. We were constantly scouting out our next location, negotiating lodging, packing and unpacking. Plus, there was a ton of stuff to see and do in every place; there was little downtime. So finding three or four hours to focus on work was nearly impossible.

The end result was that I returned home without any of the plans and legwork that I had hoped to accomplish during this amazing trip. I was expecting to get a lot more writing done during the trip. I was planning to have a lot of my new business ideas hammered out and ready to execute as soon as we hit the ground in San Diego. But right when we got home we were overwhelmed with assimilating back into everyday life. So that put my work on hold for another few months.

But hey, I did write this book that you're reading!

WHAT IF WE HAD ALL THAT MONEY BACK?

One of the many discussions Jessica and I had a lot before deciding to do this trip was about finances. This is one of the most important conversations that you and your spouse must have beforehand.

Now that we're back home we've had some time to think about what the trip cost and if it was money well spent. Would we like to have all the money we spent on the trip sitting in our bank account right now? Of course! But maybe that's not the right question. The real question boiled down to this: if we could go back in time and cancel the trip and keep the money, would we do it? Would we give up all those incredible, once-in-a-lifetime memories? Would we give up all that incredible family bonding time?

I think you know what my answer here is going to be. Absolutely no way! It was the best money I ever spent. Period.

"How many times have you thought back on a trip and said, 'I regret that experience and wish I had my money back?'"

Before we left on our sabbatical we knew it was going to be expensive. I remember asking Jessica, "Out of every trip we've ever taken, which one do you regret?" She said, "None. I don't regret a single trip we've ever taken." That's what I thought. I said, "If you could have the money back from any of those trips, which one would you take?" She said, "None." And that's one of the reasons we decided to do this trip. I think we both agree that every trip we've ever taken was worth every penny. Neither one of us would trade in those experiences just to have some money back in our bank account. We knew we'd never regret it. We shared something amazing with our children that very few families get to do.

💬 LONDON OMG! MOMENT

You may recall from earlier in this book that I lost $1 million in this city during the 2012 Olympics. But on this trip I realized I walked around and saw more in a single day than I had seen spending one miserable month there three years ago. Mindset matters so much when you're traveling.

💬 LONDON LOL! MOMENT

Toward the end of the evening in London, the last night of our trip before heading home, we got ice cream. Blaise was so focused on eating it and he walked face first into a pole. Everyone (except him) thought this was pretty funny. He had ice cream running down his face as he yelled at everyone for laughing at him. But what I took away from that story is that kids are great at living in the moment. Blaise was 100% in the moment and focused on eating that ice cream.

And that's one of the great lessons of taking a year-long sabbatical with your family. You will learn to live in the moment in a way that may be impossible for you right now. I promise this will change your life for the better. After all, what else do we have but this very moment right here, right now?

* * *

I'd love to hear from you! If you're considering taking an epic voyage like the one described in this book, please reach out to me. Let's chat. I'd love to hear more about your trip and even help you plan it. I'm always happy to answer questions on this topic. Or if you'd like me to come speak at your school, company or organization, I'd love to do it. I have lectured widely on this topic and I can promise a fascinating multimedia presentation that will fascinate, educate, and inspire your audience.

I hope to hear from you. God speed, and safe travels!

Adam

adamdailey@gmail.com

@KeepMovingFast

"*The life you have led doesn't need to be the only life you have.*"

— ANNA QUINDLEN

FULL ITINERARY WITH TRAVEL COSTS

THE TASK OF KEEPING TRACK of a year's worth of expenses on a trip can be tedious. Many of our big expenses (airfare, lodging) we were able to buy with frequent flier miles and points. But I did take a stab at estimating the total cost of the trip. Below is a breakdown of each leg and the associated costs. You'll find more information about the total cost at the end of this section.

COSTA RICA

Flights from Austin, Texas, to Costa Rica
We used Air Canada frequent flyer miles and the flights were cheap since they were one-way trips (around 15,000 miles per flight). To purchase the flight would have cost around $250 each, one way. Total for a family of six, $1,500.

Accommodations for six in Costa Rica

We were there for a month and spent a total of $3500, so a little more than $100 per day. We stayed in some amazing properties along the way:

We stayed at Casa Mono Titi (http://www.casamonotiti.com) in Manuel Antonio (about $100 a night for a huge house, with cleaning, pool and monkeys).

We stayed at a three-bedroom condo resort with pool in Nosara, Costa Rica, right on Playa Pelada for $1000 for 12 nights. Approximately $84 per night.

Then we stayed in a VRBO rental at Playa Junquillal (https://www.vrbo.com/335234) for $927 for 8 nights. $116 per night.

After that, we drove over to the town of Arenal, which was a long haul. I bargained with the Green Lagoon Hotel (a #1 rated hotel on TripAdvisor) to give us a luxury two-bedroom suite with our own private pool for $500 for 3 nights. $167 per night.

Our last night we stayed at the Hampton Inn at the San Jose airport since we had an early morning flight. We used miles to stay at this hotel for free for the last night.

Food for six in Costa Rica for a month

In Costa Rica we would make runs to the grocery store wherever we were and load up. We would also have nice dinners at one of the three restaurants in Nosara (Olga's, Il Pepperoni, or La Luna) and it would run $35-50 for all of us. It was also great that all places had open space where the kids could run around and play.

VANCOUVER

Flights from Costa Rica to Vancouver

We booked flights from Costa Rica to Vancouver for 12,500 miles per person on American Airlines, which was a good deal. But it was a really long day of traveling. We had a five-hour layover in Dallas, but we were able to go to Jessica's brother's house and swim and see family during that time, so we made the best of it. We also made some wardrobe changes during our short time in the USA, where everything is cheaper.

The flights would have cost around $350 per person, or $2,100 total.

Accommodations for six in Vancouver for about five weeks

In total we spent $3,000 Canadian dollars (about $2,700 USD at the time) plus three nights in Whistler at $50 a night. We found a three-bedroom small home in the Commercial Drive area of Vancouver, which is where we lived from 2008 to 2010. It was quite the opposite experience of our time in Costa Rica. Not only did we need our jackets when we arrived, but we were in a very urban setting for the first time in a month. We found a great deal by sending many emails and then negotiating; most of the other properties were almost twice as much. The landlord, Laurie, lived below us so we saw her often. The boys always said nice things about her. "We miss Laurie," was a strange sentiment we'd hear as we were out exploring Vancouver (and once we left it).

Food for six in Vancouver for five weeks

Vancouver was more expensive than almost anywhere else we went, largely because of the cost of food. Lunches would cost more than $10 a person plus tax and tip (with the strange exception being that sushi is cheap in

Vancouver). And taxes are high with both GST and PST (think double sales tax!). So we didn't eat out that much here, since it was a pretty shocking contrast to our experience in Costa Rica.

Living in Vancouver was similar to being in the USA (they have Costco, chain restaurants, etc.). The area had great markets for everything we needed, fresh produce, ravioli, cheese, etc.

We rented a minivan three different times in order to get a weekly rate because it ended up being cheaper that way. Minivans are always hard to find. This was hard for our family since we must have a minivan. We can't fit into a normal car with all of our car seats for the kids.

CALIFORNIA

SAN FRANCISCO/NAPA/SANTA BARBARA/ DISNEYLAND/SAN DIEGO

Flights from Vancouver to San Francisco

We booked a multiple trip itinerary on American Airlines in April 2014 that only cost us 50,000 miles per person for the following legs:

+ Vancouver to San Francisco
+ San Diego to Hawaii
+ Hawaii to Auckland, New Zealand

Shortly after this, American Airlines changed the rules for awards and layovers, and we actually had to talk to a supervisor to get this itinerary booked for only 50,000 miles per person, since the rule began between the time we held the reservation and booked it.

We could have flown from Vancouver to San Francisco for about $250 each (assuming we booked 2-3 months in advance). Probably more like $450-500 if its last minute. The trip to Hawaii would have been $600 per person at least. And to get to Auckland would have probably been another $600-$800 per person.

Accommodations for six in San Francisco/Northern California for 10 days
We flew in to San Francisco and got there at night. We then drove straight to Napa. We hit a Wal-Mart en-route to get an extra booster seat for Blaise (that we ended up storing in California when we left for Hawaii).

We stayed in an Embassy Suites hotel in Napa and used about 40,000 miles for three nights. It would have cost around $250+ per night otherwise, or $800 total. We used Starwood Points to book two nights at a nice hotel in downtown San Francisco (30,000 total Starwood Points, 7,500 per room per night). We had two adjoining rooms, which was a unique hotel experience.

Our friend who used to nanny for us was getting married in San Francisco. So we had committed months earlier to attend her wedding. We used miles to book hotels in Napa as well as San Francisco. So that saved money, but staying in hotel rooms was quite the contrast, and obviously limited our space.

From San Francisco, we rented a car and drove south toward Santa Barbara. We opted to take the scenic route thinking our kids would enjoy driving down the famous Pacific Coast Highway. They didn't. They had their noses in their iPads and barely looked out the window. We would come upon some of the most beautiful views of the ocean, but I think the kids missed most of them.

We spent a few days in Santa Barbara and celebrated Jett's 5th birthday with my Aunt Lynn, who lived there. We stayed in a two-bedroom suite in Santa Barbara at the Sandpiper Hotel for about $190 per night. The motel was a little run down, but included breakfast, which always ended up being a big savings for our family. Even if the breakfast was mediocre, it was a good start to the day. Plus, not having to clean up after yourself (in a hotel breakfast vs. breakfast in your kitchen at home) is always worth something.

From Santa Barbara we spent a couple of days at Disneyland in Anaheim, which the kids of course loved. We got down to San Diego by that Friday to meet my parents. They had flown in from Austin to meet us.

We got to go to Disneyland for free because of a mutual friend who worked at the Häagen-Dazs store at Disneyland. This saved us $600 for the day! Using connections to your advantage is a big piece of the puzzle. There is no harm in emailing people ahead of time and asking them to meet up, and recommend things to do with the family. You'd be surprised how often people want to help out. Our hotel is Anaheim was within walking distance of Disneyland and costs $140 per night for a two bedroom suite.

We rented the van for two weeks for about $600, which was a really great deal for a minivan (especially given that it was a one-way rental). We booked it through Costco Travel a few months in advance. This was one of the best deals of the trip. I think we got it for about half price.

We only spent nine nights in San Diego. We hadn't been back since we left in August 2013, but we also knew that we'd most likely end up moving back there after our sabbatical.

We own a house there that we rent full time on Airbnb in San Diego. We were excited about staying there during our time in San Diego, but a couple weeks before someone inquired and offered to pay $500 a night to stay there. That was great for us financially, but it meant we needed a place to stay!

So even though we owned two houses in San Diego, we ended up renting a beach house in Mission Beach for about $2000 (around $225 a night). It was a splurge.

Travel from San Francisco to San Diego

We drove from San Francisco to San Diego in about 5 days. It was a little rushed, but we stopped in Monterey, Carmel, Santa Barbara (where we celebrated Jett's birthday) and Disneyland. Awesome road trip, but I would recommend taking weeks, not days, to do this same journey.

We had to meet my parents on a Friday in San Diego because those were the flights they had booked. It made me realize it's hard when you *have* to be somewhere at an exact time. I much prefer flexibility.

Food for six in San Diego for nine days

We had BBQs and we knew good restaurants and markets, and we had my parents in town for a few days. So it was about the same cost as traveling to most cities in the USA. We are exceptional at being able to go to a pretty good restaurant and spend only about $50 to $60 for our whole family ($15 on adult beverages, three entrees at $12 each, and maybe an appetizer).

HAWAII

Flights from San Diego

As noted, we used one frequent flier award to book Vancouver to San Francisco to San Diego to Hawaii to Auckland for 50,000 miles per person.

Accommodations for six in Hawaii for five days

We were in Hawaii for five nights. We used miles to pay for the hotel (about 103,000 British Airways miles). It would have cost us around $350+ a night if we had paid out of pocket, or $1,750.

Food for six in Hawaii for five days

Hawaii is generally expensive, but they still adhere to the USA 'Happy Hour' custom, so we took advantage of that. We ate at the Yard House two times and got tons of happy hour food and beer for about $50. Same thing at P.F. Changs. We had a crappy breakfast that was free at the hotel every day. But overall, we generally found food to be pretty cheap for us in Hawaii. We also found an amazing Udon noodle place (Marukame Udon) that was super casual but probably one of the best meals on the entire trip. We went there twice.

NEW ZEALAND

Accommodations for six in New Zealand for seven weeks

We were in New Zealand for seven weeks and spent a total of $3800 on lodging. That works out to less than $80 per day. We used miles to book a hotel in Wellington (2 nights) and Queenstown for our last 5 nights, which were an amazing ending to such a great country.

We booked a place in Pt. Chevalier in Auckland for about 15 nights for $2000 NZD. It was a former beach house right on the water and was truly an amazing experience. We had to be super flexible with the dates because the owner actually lived there and was leaving town. So we got to Auckland, explored, then traveled for about 10 days, then came back. We were at the beach (our yard) every single day and the view was truly amazing.

Food for six in New Zealand

We felt like Auckland had pretty mediocre restaurants that were overpriced. So we didn't eat out as often. We hit the grocery stores (Countdown and World Market) and cooked meals at our houses throughout the North and South Island. The cost of groceries was about the same as in the USA. Kiwis like to BBQ, so we were always up for grilling meat.

AUSTRALIA

SYDNEY, AUSTRALIA
Flights from New Zealand to Sydney
We booked our Queenstown to Sydney flight on Qantas, but using American Airlines miles. It only set us back 10,000 miles per person (plus a $70 booking fee). This later incurred a change fee as we changed our departure city from Christchurch to Queenstown. In fact, we were going to skip Queenstown altogether just due to time. I'm grateful for because Christchurch sucked and Queenstown ruled.

Flights were priced at around $300 to $400 when we looked (90 days out), but I think you could probably find airfare for $150 if you booked well in advance.

Accommodations for six in Sydney for five weeks
We were in Sydney for about five weeks and that place cost us $5300, or roughly $150 per day. This was more expensive than anywhere else on our trip, but it was an awesome deal for Sydney. We had many places trying to charge us $2000 to $3000 for just New Year's Eve!

Food for six in Sydney for five weeks
We went out a lot in Australia. We found reliable babysitters everywhere in the major cities (Sydney, Melbourne, etc.). And we could maneuver around the country pretty easily because we knew the language.

We'd go out for dinner with our whole family and spend about $60 to $70 on average. We discovered a great Domino's deal pizza as well, good-sized medium pizzas for $5.00, and the kids loved it. Yes, I realized getting a couple Domino's pizzas aren't the most cultured thing to talk about when you're discussing a trip around the world. But hey, family members require a lot of picnics and other improvisational meals.

AUSTRALIA

Accommodations for six in Australia for ten weeks

We spent about $11,000 on lodging for a total of three and a half months in Australia. That averages out to about $105 per day. Sydney was more expensive than most anywhere else in the country.

For the most part, we spent about $100 a day for our accommodations in Australia. We got lucky that we had friends who let us stay at their amazing place in the Mornington Peninsula (in a small town called Rye), south of Melbourne, for a week for free—and their house was awesome. We also had other friends outside of Melbourne that let us stay with them for about four or five nights during the time of the Melbourne Grand Prix Formula One race. It is always complicated when your trip coincides with a special event. But it's also really fun. When you're staying for a month, you can avoid paying skyrocketed prices by negotiating a lower long-term rate. But when you're staying just a week or less, you really lose your leverage. When we went back to Melbourne it was the weekend of the Ironman competition, so once again it was tough to find lodging that wasn't super expensive.

Food for six in Australia for ten weeks

We found Australia to be expensive, but not crazy expensive. And the quality was pretty good. Coffees were expensive, but we did a ton of grocery shopping throughout Australia to keep costs down on a daily basis.

THAILAND

Flights from Sydney to Thailand

We spent 35,000 American Airlines miles per person to fly Business Class to Bangkok. This flight would have cost more than $2,000 I'm sure, and probably $600 to $700 to fly in economy.

All along, we had planned to come back to Sydney to get the flight. But then we realized how much we were enjoying Melbourne. Remember the part about flexibility? So instead of cutting out time in Melbourne, we each paid an extra $150 change fee to leave out of Melbourne. This meant we would be on our same flight to Bangkok from Sydney. We basically just added on a flight back there for $150 each, which we would have had to buy anyway. It was nice to have access to the first class lounge, but the long travel day was not such a luxurious experience. The main problem was that after a long day of traveling to Bangkok, we had to go outside, recheck our bags and wait for a couple hours for our flight to Phuket. Zane cried the entire time.

Accommodations for six in Thailand for two weeks

We booked a two-bedroom apartment suite at Casuarina Shores for about $1400 for twelve nights, or $117 per night. I was able to negotiate about 40% off. We booked a two-bedroom luxury apartment at Somerset Lake Point Bangkok for $135 per night via booking.com.

Food for six in Thailand for two weeks

In Phuket we would spend around $25 to $30 on a meal for lunch and dinner for the whole family. This was really consistent. If we splurged (had more beers, smoothies for every kid, etc.) it could push the tab closer to $40. We also found a great restaurant called Pesto that was amazing.

SPAIN

Flights from Thailand to Spain in miles

This leg cost us 61,000 Capital One miles per person. But this particular card gives you 2 miles per dollar spent, so it was really like 30,000 miles per person. This was a good deal for such a long flight, but the miles are based on market/cash value. By booking in advance, we saved more miles. The good thing about the flight was the total travel time, which was minimal.

Normal price would have been around $700 each. We flew to Helsinki, had a brief layover, then gave our kids some Benadryl and they passed out from Finland to Barcelona. I'm sure everyone on the plane was wondering how four kids could sleep during the entire flight at 5 p.m. This is probably another moment where other parents would disapprove of our tactics. But after the dreadful Australia to Thailand flight, we wanted to do whatever we could to make things easier for everyone.

Accommodations for six in Barcelona for five weeks

We rented two different flats. One in the l'Eixample district for two weeks for about $100 a day. We booked another flat in the Born, right next to the house we lived in during 2007 and 2008. It was huge (five bedrooms) for Spain and it cost 2000 euros for 23 nights, less than 90 Euros per night. That was and still is a great deal for Barcelona. The flat was about 80 meters from the home where we'd lived when Chiara was born.

Food for six in Barcelona for five weeks

Because our flats were relatively small (by American standards), it was never that comfortable to cook (or clean up) at home, so we'd do like the Europeans and usually get out for at least one meal a day. We were amazed at how cheap Spain was. Cups of amazing coffee (café con leche) were barely $1. We could sit down and have beers with four or five tapas plates —enough to almost feed everyone—for less than 25 euros. We rarely felt the need to do much more than that for dinner. We would go out almost daily to have coffee (for the adults) and pastries (for the little guys) on some amazing square (plaza) for the equivalent of about five bucks.

Accommodations for six in Spain for two weeks
We found a great place (Smart Suites Albaicin) on Booking.com in Granada for about $100 a night. From there, we had a modern flat in the great Santa Cruz Barrio of Seville that was only about $75 or $80 a day. The Seville home was so nice we extended our trip by a couple of days there and cut out more time in Madrid. That's an example of the benefits of not having booked everything in advance. Our place in Madrid (Hotel Gran Via Suites) was also less than $125 a day for a nice three-bedroom perfectly located.

Food for six in Spain for two weeks
We found Southern Spain to be even cheaper than Barcelona. Plus, there were lots of places where you could go and order a beer in the afternoon and they would give you a free appetizer. We would typically spend between 20 to 35 Euros per meal. But we also did tapas almost exclusively and rarely sat down for a full meal anywhere we went during the trip.

The only exception would be a meal we had in Madrid at an upscale tapas restaurant on a Sunday afternoon. Zane was sleeping in his stroller (a rarity) and we took advantage of the situation with three kids; it was amazing. By this point, our one-year-old had almost become a two-year-old, and he was becoming a restaurant terror.

FRANCE

Flights from Spain To France

Tickets cost $65 each from Madrid to Paris. And we got free food and drinks on the flight!

Problem was there was a wreck on the highway from the airport to our hotel. The information person at the airport dissuaded us from taking the metro to Central Paris because of our kids and bags. So we took a taxi and the trip took close to two hours. Zane lost it and I couldn't blame him. In the end, I think the taxi ride cost 100 Euros and we were about an hour late checking into our flat in Central Paris.

Accommodations for six in France for a week

We paid 850 euros (around $925) for a week in a small two-bedroom apartment in Central Paris, or about $132 per night. It was a great experience overall. Quarters were tight, but we were out for most of the day.

Food for six in France for a week

We had been to Paris more than ten times in our lives and we knew not to skimp on food when in the City of Light. While the French aren't recognized globally for being nice, they sure know how to eat. We ended up going to Sacré-Coeur twice and doing picnics up there—the view of Paris was incredible, and overall atmosphere is great for kids (music, grass, etc.). The kids loved that, other than the street peddlers everywhere trying to scam us. We did find it a lot more expensive than Spain, however. But the food in Paris was worth every Euro. Count on lots of picnics and street food. The delis and markets, of course, have amazing cheese and breads. But for a proper sit down type of meal, it was hard to spend less than 100 euros. Again, you don't want to skimp on food while in France.

ITALY

Travel from France To Italy

We took a train from Paris to Torino for about 35 Euros per person. This was a good move because it departed from the center of town in Paris and arrived at the center of town in Torino. That's the big advantage of trains --not having to mess with airports and costly ground transportation.

Accommodations for six in Italy for three weeks

We spent about $125 a day, $2800 total. It was more expensive than the other places we'd been visiting, but we had amazing villas that were normally twice the price. For us, it was about leveraging deals. While we tried to stay at $100 a night throughout the trip, I was always interested in a $1500 a night opportunity if I could get it for $250. We also had a great deal in Rome (less than $100 per night) for a four-bedroom place right by the Vatican.

Food for six in Italy for three weeks

Like France, we were not going to skimp on food in Italy. We ate great for the most part. We would spend around 50 to 60 Euros for a nice dinner at a restaurant and we would usually do a picnic during the day. For breakfast, we'd have cereal at home but almost always try to get out to have a coffee somewhere and get the kids a pastry of some sort. This would cost $5 (for a couple coffees and a 2-3 pastries) in Barcelona, while probably closer to $7-8 throughout Italy. While that doesn't seem like much of a difference, it was more than 50% higher.

GREECE

Flights from Italy to Greece

These flights were a bargain at only $70 USD per person. Why use miles or points when the cash price is so cheap! Again, these types of low cost European flights are non-refundable and its usually very costly to try to change them.

Accommodations for six in Greece for three weeks

We got great accommodations in the Greek islands for about $100 per day. In total we spent $2700 (for about three weeks). It helped that our friend owned a hotel in Athens (Hotel Art Gallery, right by the Acropolis). Remember how I mentioned how important connections are when it comes to traveling?

Mykonos was the most expensive, and crowded, and overall not the best choice for us. But there weren't many direct flights out of the islands to Europe. And it was our fault for visiting Mykonos in high season.

Food for six in Greece for three weeks

The food in Greece was amazing, and overall pretty good prices. We would order our staple of typical dishes—Greek salad, calamari, fried eggplant, Saganaki cheese, etc.) Those were about $7 each. I loved drinking Mythos beer which cost about two euros in most places. We ate out most of the time because it was inexpensive and delicious. Our meals would run between 32 and 45 euros. The definition of Greek breakfast is coffee and cigarettes. They're not known for breakfast, so we'd eat at our place in the mornings.

GERMANY

Flights from Greece to Germany

We used 12,500 American Airlines miles per person to get from Mykonos to Munich. I think the flight would have cost around $400 per person (probably half of that if we'd have booked 4-6 months in advance). Our itinerary had us down for a two-hour layover in Vienna, but we were able to push back our departure until the next morning. That was great because Jessica was able to connect with her friend from graduate school and spend the evening with her in Vienna. This was the only night we split up during the trip; I headed straight to Munich.

Unfortunately, when we got to Munich, my two little guys were fried and they didn't have our stroller; the airline lost it. So managing Zane without being able to contain him in a stroller was *really* hard. Remember what I said about rolling with the punches? He was loopy, just a couple days shy of being two years old (when you have to start buying the kids a plane ticket). Yes, by the way, I planned his last free plane ticket that way on purpose! By the time we made it to our flat in Munich, we were spent. But it was nice that Jessica could enjoy that experience in Austria.

Accommodations for six in Germany for two weeks

This cost about $2250 for twelve nights, or about $188 per night. Germany is not a cheap place, but we got some killer deals. It could have cost twice that much. We rented a two-bedroom flat in Munich for less than $200 a night, half the price of every other listing online.

Food for six in Germany for two weeks

Again, food was expensive—and not very good, to be honest. But we were at the end of our trip, and we wanted to ensure we'd have a great time. If we ate at a restaurant, it was hard to get out of there for less than 50 euros.

LONDON

Flights from Dusseldorf to London and back to the USA

We spent 50,000 miles per ticket to get from Dusseldorf to the USA. This was a business class flight, however, and it was a pretty way to end an amazing trip! When that flight touched down, we didn't want to get off the plane. And we were allowed up to a 24-hour layover without paying extra. We were scheduled to leave Dusseldorf at 6:30 in the morning and fly straight back to Austin, but we decided to change our tickets and leave the day before so we could spend a day in London.

Accommodations for six in London

We used 20,000 miles per room for two rooms to stay at an airport hotel near Heathrow.

Food for six in London

We spent $100 at a noodle place that was pretty nice. It was one of our most expensive meals of the trip. But Zane and the boys were acting horrible and Jessica had to take Zane on a walk half way through dinner.

UNITED STATES

When we finally landed back in the United State, I felt a range of emotions. I felt a sense of pride. We'd done it! I felt relief—everyone was safe and healthy. I felt sad. For the past 12 months, every day was an adventure. Things wouldn't be like that going forward.

TOTAL COST OF THE TRIP

Our accommodations ending up costing less than $40,000 for the year. What do you spend on your home? Not just the mortgage, but also insurance, maintenance, your cable and electric bill? The accommodations were the largest expense of the trip for us. While our home costs were about $100+ per day, food was less, and total transportation costs were less than $6000 for the trip (cars, buses, etc.; not flights).

TRIP COSTS (FOR OUR FAMILY OF SIX)

Place	Daily Accomodations	Notes	Daily Food	Notes
Costa Rica	$110		$60	
Vancouver	$90	Great deal on a house	$60	Mostly Groceries
California	$140	Splurged on beach house	$75	USA is pricey!
Hawaii	$0	Used Miles	$80	
New Zealand	$90		$55	Lots of groceries
Sydney	$140	High season	$70	
Australia	$95	Two friends' places (free)	$80	Lots of picnics
Thailand	$125	Luxury	$60	Lunch and Dinner out
Spain	$100		$60	
Paris, France	$125	Great but small 2BR flat	$85	Don't skimp in France
Italy	$140			
Greece	$135	Free Athens Hotel	$75	Lunch and Dinner Out
Germany	$140	High season	$65	Beer + Picnics

Another note about expenses; it's like keeping your journal. Its tedious but can be worth it as you analyze things (budgeted vs. actual expenses). You will notice I got a little lazy towards the end of our trip. Paying with credit cards certainly helps preserve record keeping a little bit better.

THE GRAND TOTAL

If you would like to know the exact and specific costs of our trip, including the grand total cost of the year, please visit our website KeepMovingFast. com. There is a downloadable spreadsheet there that has a ton of detail. If you're considering taking your own sabbatical, I recommend you study our numbers.

I also would love to hear from you and learn about your plans. Contact me at this email address *adamdailey@gmail.com*.

ABOUT THE AUTHOR

ADAM DAILEY's history as a professional athlete, entrepreneur, sports marketer, traveler and speaker, shows that he has always followed his passion. It's what drove him to spend a year traveling the world with his family in tow.

Dailey inspires others to change their lives through travel. He is the co-founder of FunLy Events, the managing director at Keep Moving Fast, and founder of Beer Marketing. Dailey and his family call La Jolla, California their home base.